SIDDHARTHA BOSE

Siddhartha Bose's books include two poetry collections, *Kalagora* and *Digital Monsoon* (Penned in the Margins, 2010 & 2013), and a monograph on the grotesque, *Back and Forth* (Cambridge Scholars Publishing, 2015). He has been featured on BBC Four, BBC Radio 3 and BBC Asian Network, and was dubbed one of the 'ten rising stars of British poetry' by *The Times*. Sid's theatre work include *Kalagora*, *London's Perverted Children*, long-listed for an Oxford Samuel Beckett Theatre Trust award, and *The Shroud*. He has made a film on Mumbai, *Animal City*, and guest-edited a special issue of the literary journal *Wasafiri* (Routledge, UK/USA) on international urban writing. Siddhartha was a Leverhulme Fellow in Drama at Queen Mary, University of London (2011-13). He is an Associate Artist at Penned in the Margins, and currently teaches at Global Shakespeare (QMUL/Warwick). He lives in London.

No Dogs, No Indians

Siddhartha Bose

Penned in the Margins

LONDON

PUBLISHED BY PENNED IN THE MARGINS
Toynbee Studios, 28 Commercial Street, London E1 6AB
www.pennedinthemargins.co.uk

The right of Siddhartha Bose to be identified as the author of this work has been asserted by him in accordance with Section 77 of the Copyright, Designs and Patent Act 1988.

First published 2017

Printed in the United Kingdom by Bell & Bain of Glasgow

ISBN
978-1-908058-48-5

No Dogs, No Indians was co-commissioned by Brighton Festival, Southbank Centre, Live Theatre, GemArts, Writers' Centre Norwich & Norwich Arts Centre; produced by Penned in the Margins; and supported with public funding by Arts Council England. The script was developed with Russell Bender and Tom Chivers.

First performed on 17th May 2017 at Brighton Festival, followed by Southbank Centre, London as part of Alchemy Festival, Norwich Arts Centre as part of Norfolk & Norwich Festival, and Live Theatre, Newcastle as part of Masala Festival.

Cast and creative team:

Komal Amin as Pritilata 'Rani' Waddedar
Omar Khan as Shyamal, Ananda, Nirmal Sen
Ashraf Ejjbair as Yogesh, Surya Sen, Biswas, Bahadur
Archana Ramaswamy as Chorus, Durga, Kalpana

Russell Bender Director
Mila Sanders Designer
Jai Morjaria Lighting Designer
Edward Lewis Sound Designer
Lauren Cameron Company Stage Manager
Tom Chivers Producer

No Dogs,
No Indians

The chained dog, being a dog, whines and sometimes barks
This being his constitutional right: he lives on leftovers;
He's used to injustice; his mind is desensitised;
He'd be shot dead if he took a chance to rebel and break free of his chain.
Every street resounds with the drum of 'Total Liberation'.
Friends, I ask an uncircumcised child what democracy means,
What you eat it with.

— NAMDEO DHASAL

for Indra

CHARACTERS

1931-32	Pritilata 'Rani' Waddedar
	Kalpana Dutta
	Ramkrishna Biswas
	Surya Sen
	Nirmal Sen
	Three revolutionaries
1970s	Shyamal Chatterjee
	Durga Chatterjee
	Bahadur
2017	Ananda Chatterjee
	Yogesh
	Ruksana
	Chorus

ACT I

SCENE 1

2017. A Bombay skyscraper, overlooking the sea and the new skyline of the city. Ananda Chatterjee, a man in his thirties, is visiting from London. He's with his old friends, Yogesh and Ruksana. Yogesh wears a sleeveless t-shirt and frayed blue jeans. Ruksana's in jeans and a kurti. She fixes a whiskey. Yogesh snorts a line of cocaine on a glass table. Offers to Ananda, who's dressed in black. Ananda accepts, snorts, coughs.

YOGESH. Good shit, haan? Get good stuff in England?

ANANDA. Nice. Nahi yaar, I lead a boring, boring life. Work and nothing else.

RUKSANA. Whadddare you sayin', Ananda, you live abroad, na?

YOGESH. Arre, screw 'abroad', yaar. You're lucky to be here, Ananda. Bombay's where it's at. Money and movies. There are more skyscrapers being built here than anywhere else in the world, boss!

RUKSANA. Oh come off that Discovery Channel bullshit, Yogesh! You want a whiskey, Ananda? Don't listen to him. He talks like this when he's all coked up.

ANANDA. Which is pretty much all the time, na?

RUKSANA. That's Bombay. The city is drowning in a hail of cocaine.

YOGESH. Arre, even cabbies in Bombay are snorting cola, boss!

ANANDA. Where's it all coming from? Yah Ruksi, I'll have another—

YOGESH. *(cutting another line)* How should I know? Colombia, via the US, via Amsterdam, all the way to aamchi Mumbai? The globalisation of dope, yaar. You should write an article on it.

RUKSANA. Ya seriously, Ananda, what do you write about?

ANANDA. Leave it, guys!

RUKSANA. Arre tell us, no! What? You think we're too dumb, haan?

ANANDA. Stuff about Independence movements. Our independence movements. Indian Republican Army, violent uprisings, that sort of thing.

Yogesh and Ruksi look at each other and burst into laughter.

What's so funny, guys? Somebody's got to—c'mon guys.

YOGESH. Shit yaar, you Non-Resident Indians are way too serious! Bloody NRIs! Nobody in India gives a shit about this stuff anymore, gandu!

RUKSANA. Maybe we should, Yogi!

YOGESH. Gimme my blow and I'll care about anything! Shit, I should ask my Nigerian where he gets it. Next time, promise!

ANANDA. What?

RUKSANA. Thomas, he's the one who brings it over.

ANANDA. What are you talking about, chooth?

YOGESH. The cola, chooth!

ANANDA. Home delivery?

RUKSANA. Like everything else in Bombay, baby. Don't have to lift a finger. Just gotta have the rokra to spend. Splash the cash, and watch the fun! Yaar, it's been so long, Ananda! Look at you! All tip-top British gent and all.

YOGESH. Ya, walking around with a stick up his ass!

ANANDA. I didn't think you'd hook up with this fool, Ruksi.

RUKSANA. Didn't have much of a choice!

YOGESH. It's good to see you, bro.

ANANDA. Like being back in college.

YOGESH. Good old days! Let's snort away!

RUKSANA. Started already, haan?

ANANDA. What's this crap about "your Nigerian"?

RUKSANA. What?

ANANDA. "Your Nigerian"?

YOGESH. Yah, so?

ANANDA. Nothing, things are different here.

YOGESH. Whaddareyou saying bhenchod!? Speak clearly no. Going round and round in circles and all like a bloody auto stuck in traffic.

RUKSANA. Ya, stop mumbling Ananda. Open your heart and say what you want to say.

ANANDA. You guys should be in Bollywood.

RUKSANA. Don't worry yaar, one day, even that'll happen.

ANANDA. You look like you've done okay for yourself, Yogi.

YOGESH. Business is good, yaar, can't complain.

ANANDA. Ruksi?

RUKSANA. Haan?

ANANDA. Work?

RUKSANA. I'm selling soap yaar. And everything else under the sun. Insurance, cars, cricket, mobile phones, 3g, 4g, 5g, you know? Usual advertising shit—

YOGESH. Customer is king!

RUKSANA. This country's full of idiots. The trick is to figure out how to make money off them. And ya, if you work hard enough, you can make anything happen in this city. (beat) Arre, you know Swedish House Mafia, ya?

ANANDA. Who?

RUKSANA. Don't tell me—

YOGESH. Arre, I bet he only listens to jazz!

RUKSANA. Doesn't matter. So, they were touring India last month. You know, all over, Delhi, Bangalore, Bombay, Goa.

ANANDA. No Cal?

RUKSANA. Calcutta's stuck in the past, sweetie. Been left behind. The British have left. Foreign folks have bigger fish to fry.

YOGESH. *(yawning)* Oye Ruksi, roll a doobie, na?

RUKSANA. You do it!

YOGESH. Spicy! Chal...

Yogesh starts emptying a smoke, rolling a spliff.

RUKSANA. So where was I?

ANANDA. Swedish something—

RUKSANA. Ya, Swedish House Mafia. The chaos starts from the moment they land. They bring their own security, but they don't realise this is India. Things work differently here—

YOGESH. Listen to this—

ANANDA. I'm trying—

RUKSANA. We're in Taj land's end in Bandra, right? So these gores with their security people, they're kind of, you know, throwing their weight around. 'We got to vet everything, the journalists, the food, the vibes, the hotel, everything.' At some point, things kick off. I work with this guy called Aman. Delhi dude, carries a gun, and he won't think twice about blowing your brains out if you mess with him. Aman was like, you know guys, *we'll* decide what happens here. And then a Swedish security guy pushes Aman, okay? And that's it! Aman takes the gun out, waves it around in this posh hotel, in the lobby, you know, and the Swedes are screaming like schoolkids, and then he just kicks the entire lot out of the hotel!

ANANDA. No!

RUKSANA. Ya, man. You've got these A-list European musicians sitting outside Bandstand, middle of the day, not knowing where to go. They were all forced to apologise to Aman. That security guy had to get down on his knees, yaar, I kid you not!

YOGESH. That evening, they're all tweeting about how India's the greatest country in the world etc etc. That's how they got back into the hotel, boss.

ANANDA. You guys are totally coked!

RUKSANA. Best thing was the gig in Goa. So there's Sunburn and a bunch of other fests happening around the same time. The whole world's there. Everyone's high as hell. Nobody can do shit. The cops have been bought, ya?

ANANDA. Sounds like paradise.

YOGESH. Arre, shut up and listen, na!

RUKSANA. And I'm organising gigs in the midst of this madness.

YOGESH. And Aman's with his gangster friends, you know, the type who pull their guns out if the DJ plays the wrong tune, ya?

RUKSANA. I gotta manage all the different stages, all the equipment, like if someone says they need a subwoofer, like a Yamaha DXS12, I gotta make sure it's there. Simple as that. We're working 24/7, and the only way we can do it is with a shitload of cola!

YOGESH. And after three days, all the cola we brought over from Bombay's done, yaar. So what do we do?

RUKSANA. I make Yogesh call Thomas.

YOGESH. 'My Nigerian,' yah?

ANANDA. Uh-huh.

RUKSANA. And Yogesh calls Thomas and says —

YOGESH. 'Bro, we need you man, we need another ten grams, you gotta come to Goa, right now, asap, we'll bloody pay for your train, bro.'

ANANDA. (laughing) You guys are crazy!

RUKSANA. And I kid you not, the next day he's in Goa —

YOGESH. But check this out, ya? The chooth doesn't just want to deal, he wants to party as well, so —

RUKSANA. Shut up, Yogi, my story —

YOGESH. Sorry yaar.

RUKSANA. So, he's in bloody Goa and I'm waiting for him, you know, and Thomas arrives, he gets out of the cab and —

YOGESH. Mad gandu!

RUKSANA. He's all dressed up in a suit, a leopard stripe suit, I kid you not, and a black hat, and he's carrying a cane, man he's got a chutiya cane with him! Just picture it, ya? You have this big African guy in the middle of Goa dressed in a leopard suit, and he says —

YOGESH. *(in a mock deep voice)* 'If I'm coming to Goa, then I'm coming to party! Yeah!'

All three friends are laughing now. The laughter builds until, suddenly, Ruksi raises her hand and the scene freezes. Yogi and Ananda are frozen in mid-laughter. Ruksi steps out of the scene and becomes Chorus.

CHORUS. Ladies and gentlemen, mesdames et messieurs, aadmis and aurats! Here I am, mother India, forever India, land of the meek, home of the slave, in yoga we trust! Yes, you see, we attained the summits of civilisation as far back as the 4th century BC, but my body bears the scars of...ghulami. Slavery. A few hundred years ago, came the fair folk. And when the fair folk with their moustaches and their leather boots and their bowler hats landed in Calcutta, they said we were nameless. Ha! What a swindle! *(beat)* From Thomas Macaulay's minute on Indian education, circa 1835 — *'We must at present do our best to form a class who may be interpreters between us and the millions whom we govern, — a class of persons Indian in blood and colour, but English in tastes, in opinions, in morals and in intellect.'* Here, here, let me give you some examples of Macaulay's great grandchildren, see see — (*she points to Ananda and Yogesh, still frozen in laughter*) — this is the lot! Indian in blood, Western in ways, foreigners in their own land! *(beat)* Take the case of our dear friend, Ananda Chatterjee here. He's just flown in from England. His father's passed away — oops! So so sorry, spoiler alert! I didn't mean to, but — poor sweetie-pie, cry me a river. His dad's died. And tell you the truth, it's his dad we're interested in.

Ananda gets up, walks downstage towards a mirror. During Chorus's words, he dresses himself up in a neatly pressed suit, cufflinks, pince-nez, polished black shoes, and fiddles with a pipe. Ananda becomes Shyamal Chatterjee, his father.

And here is our asli hero, Shyamal Chatterjee! C'mon everyone, clap for him! And as every hero must have a heroine — even if they'll never meet each other — here is Pritalata Waddeddar, or Rani as she's known to her friends, preparing to launch an attack on a whites-only club in British India.

Rani in front of a mirror, other end of stage. She is dressing herself up, slowly, as a Punjabi man, with a beard and a turban.

Great, give her a round of applause too! But don't get too excited, haan, we'll get to her later. Safe to say Rani's the type who would've been *ashamed* of Shyamal Chatterjee. Why? Let's find out. Here he is, in 1975, not in Bombay, but in Calcutta, once the second city of the British Empire.

ACT I | SCENE 2

SHYAMAL. *(examining himself in the mirror)*
  'But I, that am not shaped for sportive tricks,
  Nor made to court an amorous looking-glass;
  I, that am curtail'd of this fair proportion,
  Cheated of feature by dissembling nature,
  Deformed, unfinish'd, sent before my — '

What's the bloody line? Shit. Shit, shit. Sent before my...time? Yes. Ah the English language! O Shakespeare, master, I bow to thee!

Shyamal stares at himself in the mirror. Fixes himself a glass of whiskey. Drinks.

'But I, that am not shaped for sportive tricks'. Yes, but I, am not. Look at me!

As Shyamal continues, lights start to fade on RANI. Chorus becomes Durga and knocks on the door.

Who? Now?

He opens the door. Durga enters.

Ah, you?

DURGA. Yes, me. Why not?

SHYAMAL. Why not what?

DURGA. Why not me? I'm the one who's got to —

SHYAMAL. Can't talk now, Durga. Sorry. It's almost time for the show.

DURGA. And you want to go on stage with torn buttons, haan?

SHYAMAL. What?

DURGA. *(pointing)* Buttons. Look look, there. Shirt, pant, bloody everywhere. Here here, let me.

Durga proceeds to fix a button on Shyamal's shirt.

SHYAMAL. Thank you. What would I do without you, Durga? Dear wife!

DURGA. When does it finish?

SHYAMAL. What?

DURGA. Show.

SHYAMAL. Hmm?

DURGA. The bloody show, yaar!

SHYAMAL. How am I supposed to know? I'm an actor. I can't keep track of time.

DURGA. *(laughs)* So you're an actor, now! Arre vah, bahut khoob! Khoob bhalo!

SHYAMAL. I've got a bloody show to get through—

DURGA. Aaamlet Aaamlet! Kaun ho tum! Aaamlet Aamlet, mai tera baap ka bhoot!

SHYAMAL. English please, my dear!

DURGA. I am your father's ghost, Hamlet.

SHYAMAL. Yes, but you're a woman!

DURGA. Does it matter?

SHYAMAL. Don't get too smart, Durga.

DURGA. *(stitching button)* Bahadur was drunk again. He scares me. He's drunk all the time. You need to have a word with him.

SHYAMAL. *(sipping his drink)* I will, I promise, soon.

DURGA. You're drinking a lot these days.

SHYAMAL. What? This? It's nothing. Calms the nerves. I want to see life through an alcoholic haze!

DURGA. I'm not amused, Shyamal.

SHYAMAL. I'm sorry I failed you.

DURGA. I need some more money next month. I can't cover it all with the teaching I do. The price of fish has shot up. Meat is getting more and more expensive by the day, and I've to pay the paper man, the dhobi, the cleaner, the vegetable walla —

SHYAMAL. *(overlapping)* Not now, Durga —

DURGA. *(overlapping)* And your mother wrote saying your father's unwell, his heart's playing up again —

SHYAMAL. *(overlapping)* Of course, but now is —

DURGA. *(overlapping)* I think we should, you know, go see them sometime, really, it's been so long and —

Durga and Shyamal speaking overlaps with the sound of the stage bell, which now rings.

SHYAMAL. Quiet, Durga, please! Ten minutes, that's it! I've got to —

DURGA. Sorry.

SHYAMAL. Leave.

DURGA. What?

SHYAMAL. I need to rehearse my —

DURGA. Can't I watch?

Durga suddenly sits down, as if exhausted.

SHYAMAL. What's the matter?

DURGA. Tired.

SHYAMAL. Why?

DURGA. I want to watch.

SHYAMAL. Okay then. Watch.

Shyamal sips his whiskey, and goes back to his Shakespeare monologue.

SHYAMAL. 'But I, that am not shaped for sportive tricks,
    Nor made to court an amorous looking-glass...
    So lamely and unfashionable
    That dogs bark—'

Durga bursts into laughter.

SHYAMAL. Stop, will you!

DURGA. It's so funny, yaar.

SHYAMAL. It's Shakespeare you're laughing at.

DURGA. No no, it's—sorry—forget it.

Knock on the door.

SHYAMAL. *(shouts)* Who is it? *(beat)* Ke?

A meek and slightly drunk voice replies—'Ami dada. Jal niye eshechi.'

Enter!

No response.

Open the door please, Durga! I don't have time for this!

Durga opens the door and Bahadur enters. Bahadur places a jug of water beside Shyamal.

BAHADUR. Jal.

SHYAMAL. Thank you.

BAHADUR. Ami jayi?

SHYAMAL. Yes, you can leave.

BAHADUR. Ki?

Shyamal motions Bahadur to leave. Bahadur bows and heads towards the door, and leaves.

DURGA. He stinks of booze. *(beat)* How long has it been?

SHYAMAL. What?

DURGA. How long has he been working for us?

SHYAMAL. Bahadur? Don't know.

DURGA. He looks tired. After all these years, I still don't know what he really thinks of us.

SHYAMAL. What's so funny Durga?

DURGA. Hmm?

SHYAMAL. You were laughing, weren't you?

DURGA. *(beat)* Look at you, Shyamal. All dressed up the way you are. The accent you put on. The way you pretend to be someone you're not—

SHYAMAL. That's acting, my dear.

DURGA. You'll never be one of them, you know.

SHYAMAL. Who?

DURGA. Sahibs. White people. You don't even know who *them* is.

SHYAMAL. That's not proper English, my dear. *(beat)* And at least I'm not a bloody native.

DURGA. Of course, how could I forget? You were born in England, weren't you? It's just that... my dear, you know, you fell into the Black Sea when you were a child!

SHYAMAL. Laugh all you bloody want.

DURGA. Give me your trousers.

SHYAMAL. What?

DURGA. *(pointing)* Trousers. Buttons, zip. Take them off.

Shyamal takes off his trousers, awkwardly. He hands them over. Durga is visibly tired. She starts stitching.

SHYAMAL. You know about my Rhodes Scholarship interview, haan? Five years ago? Before our marriage? Do you even know what the Rhodes Scholarship is?

DURGA. I thought you had to rehearse your lines.

SHYAMAL. It was 1970 and I'd applied for the Rhodes Scholarship. It was a long shot, of course, but I got selected for the interview —

DURGA. *(yawns and stitches)* Really now, sweetheart, is this the moment—

SHYAMAL. It was a big deal. The interview was in Bombay. I told my father about it. He said, 'Great, take the car with you. Give yourself a few days. Drive cross- country, see it for yourself, the country you wish to leave behind.' I told him I was going to take a few friends with me. Kishore, Santu, Debu, you know, the lot. Father didn't like the idea, so I threw the car keys back at him. They either go with me, or I don't go at all, I said.

DURGA. Arre, too much! Amitabh Bachchan, proper angry young man!

SHYAMAL. I don't remember much of the journey. Two thousand kilometres. We went through small towns with names like Malegaon, Dhule, Raipur, Sambalpur. Places I'd never even heard of. We stopped and ate at the local dhabas on the highway. We drank cheap hooch. We took turns at the wheel. We—

The second bell rings.

SHYAMAL. Shit, Durga, hurry up.

DURGA. You hurry up. I need to make sure the buttons aren't loose.

SHYAMAL. We have time?

DURGA. We do. Go on.

SHYAMAL. *(beat)* We drove across the country, through all these small towns, forgotten by history, and all I remember was the ugliness of it all. The ugliness of these towns, the ugliness of the country in which I'd had the good fortune of being born in. The roads were terrible, full of potholes, and other holes *(laughs, then halts abruptly)*. In certain places, there was no bloody road at all. And if it rained, boy, you were screwed. We got stuck outside Dhule for a few hours. The road was a sea of mud, oily and thick. And all around, in the heavy rain, were broken thatched huts, unfinished homes of brick, and cow dung and mud and flies and pigs oinking away in their own shit. Factory smoke everywhere. The traffic, the horns, the anarchy, the sheer stink of it all.

DURGA. Arre vah! I didn't know you were a poet!

SHYAMAL. Shut up, Durga.

DURGA. Yes, master.

SHYAMAL. We even got into an accident near Raipur. A truck rammed into the dickey of our black Ambassador.

DURGA. You never told me this bit before.

SHYAMAL. I haven't? Lucky it was an Ambassador, haan?

DURGA. Yes. Lucky.

SHYAMAL. The lights in the back were smashed, the dickey had a dent or two. We pushed the car to the nearest karkhana, got it all spruced up, changed tyres, and continued on our way. All I remember thinking was, my god, what a shithole this country is. *(beat)* We reached Bombay after three days. And Bombay was beautiful. Or at least the old city was beautiful. The city by the sea. Foreigners had built this. Europeans, sahibs. We stayed in a rundown hotel near Colaba Causeway. The next day was interview day. At the Bombay Gymkhana. Imagine.

DURGA. How bloody English can you get?

SHYAMAL. It was afternoon. I wore my suit, the only one I had. I wore a clean, starched shirt. I wore gray flannel trousers. I wasn't nervous, but I remember feeling that something or other would go wrong. And when I sat down in one of those tiny Fiat cabs, I noticed that my trouser zip was broken.

DURGA. Oh, my poor, poor Shyamal! If only I'd been there to save you then too.

SHYAMAL. What?

Durga holds up his trousers.

(beat) I panicked. I should have just found a tailor, you know. Any tailor would have fixed the broken zip for me. But no, I panicked. I bloody panicked. My palms were sweating. I ran back to the hotel in a daze. It was humid and the sun was oppressive. I didn't have another pair of trousers. Or another suit. So I wore blue jeans, the shirt, and a blue sports jacket.

DURGA. *(laughing)* Just thinking of you in those clothes.

Shyamal starts doing his warm-ups – face, hands, arms, legs.

SHYAMAL. I was an hour late. I knew I'd blown whatever chance I had. I remember Pataudi, the cricket captain, was on the committee. He was a dashing man, you know. Handsome, princely, confident, fair. As fair as a foreigner. I don't remember the questions he asked me. I don't remember the names or the faces of the others on the panel. I barely noticed the neat wooden furniture, the sports field outside, the bearers of the club who dressed like it was still the 1930s. I was shattered inside. *(beat)*

I missed the scholarship by one point, you know. By one single bloody point. If only I'd found a tailor, that day! Life would have been different. Surely.

DURGA. *(handing him the trousers)* Good to know. I knew you never loved me.

SHYAMAL. *(wistfully)* To have gone abroad. To have walked the streets of London. My god, to have watched a Test Match at Lord's! The home of cricket!

DURGA. Oh enough, Shyamal.

SHYAMAL. Hmm?

DURGA. Wear your trousers, Shyamal.

SHYAMAL. What?

DURGA. Wear your trousers.

SHYAMAL. *(angry)* Here I am telling you everything that's ever mattered to me and —

DURGA. *(interrupting)* Stop it, will you, I'm pregnant, Shyamal. I'm going to be the mother of your child.

SHYAMAL. You can't be serious!

DURGA. Of course, I'm joking.

SHYAMAL. You are, right?

DURGA. I am going to be the mother of your child.

SHYAMAL. This is starting to sound like a bad Bombay film, you know—

DURGA. Nahi, meri jaan, this is real. Main maa banne vaali hoon. You are going to be a father. *(beat)* There, all set. Shirt, trousers, buttons. Tip-top. All done.

SHYAMAL. When did you find out?

DURGA. This afternoon.

SHYAMAL. And?

DURGA. What?

SHYAMAL. Have you told anyone else? You know I—

DURGA. *(firmly)* Grow up Shyamal. You're going to be a father.

Durga gets up. She's tired. She makes for the door.

SHYAMAL. Where the hell do you think you're going?

DURGA. Tollygunge. I'll be with my parents. I don't know when I'll come home. *(beat)* Oh, and something else—the people of this city killed for your freedom, Shyamal.

SHYAMAL. What the hell do you mean?

DURGA. Look at you!

Durga turns and leaves. Shyamal stares at himself in the mirror, finishes his whiskey. The stage bell rings.

SHYAMAL. Showtime.

ACT I | SCENE 3

CHORUS. The year is 1931. Bengal has been on fire since the Chittagong Armoury Raids of 1930, when a bunch of untrained, educated young men like Surya Sen and Nirmal Sen attacked and sabotaged the colonial machinery of Chittagong, in the northeast of occupied India. Ammunitions, railroads, trains have all been attacked. The angrez, our mighty rulers, are shitting bricks. Homes have been evacuated. The city has gone into lockdown. The angrez are on the hunt, and yet, they find nothing, no one. Meanwhile, back in Calcutta, preparations are being made for further assaults. Rani, the heroine of our story, and Ramkrishna Biswas are meeting for the first time at Alipore jail in Calcutta.

Rani and Biswas face each other.

BISWAS. *(whispers)* You're my cousin, you said?

RANI. *(whispers)* Na, your sister.

BISWAS. *(whispers)* My sister!

RANI. *(whispers)* Haan.

BISWAS. *(whispers)* Name?

RANI. Sarada.

BISWAS. What did you tell them?

RANI. That I'm married to a man from Howrah. His name is Santanu Ghosh. He's a junior barrister. A chor, a collaborator. He feels no shame in helping the British. He's ashamed that my brother is a terrorist. That you are a terrorist. I've come to meet you when he's away at work. Blood is thicker than water. *(beat)* You like it? Sarada's story?

BISWAS. *(whispers)* And you're my sister?

RANI. I am your sister.

BISWAS. *(whisper)* And they believed you?

RANI. Haan, they did.

BISWAS. Shhhh!

RANI. Sorry, Ram da, I—

BISWAS. *(aside)* They sent a woman.

RANI. What?

BISWAS. I expected someone else.

RANI. I'm sorry, I—

BISWAS. *(interrupting)* Why are you here? You're not what I— *(beat)* Who's there? Outside?

RANI. An Irishman called O'Casey. He's in charge of security. I think he hates the angrez as much as we do.

BISWAS. *(interrupting)* And the rest?

RANI. Indians. Sikhs, Muslims and a Christian man called Spanos. Even if they serve the angrez, they're still our people.

BISWAS. Greek?

RANI. Hmm?

BISWAS. Greek? Spanos.

RANI. Part Greek, part Bengali. They respect you, Ram da. They know you tried killing that horrible Craig in Chittagong.

BISWAS. Who told you? About Craig?

RANI. Our comrades. That's why I'm here.

BISWAS. Who sent you?

RANI. Nirmal. Nirmal Sen.

BISWAS. How do you know him?

RANI. He found me, Ram da.

BISWAS. Where?

RANI. Calcutta University. Indian Coffee House, just off College Street.

BISWAS. I know the Coffee House. Describe him to me?

RANI. Do we have time for this, Ram da?

BISWAS. Shh!

RANI. *(whispering)* He's quite tall. Broad shoulders. Wears glasses.

BISWAS. What does he like to eat?

RANI. Fish and rice. Cooked with mustard seeds.

BISWAS. Drink?

RANI. Haan. Whiskey.

BISWAS. A lot?

RANI. Na.

BISWAS. When did he join us?

RANI. 1928. Before the Chittagong uprising.

BISWAS. Interests?

RANI. What? *(beat)* Music.

BISWAS. What type of music?

RANI. European.

BISWAS. Books?

RANI. He reads a lot. Tagore, Conan Doyle, Shakes—

BISWAS. *(interrupting)* We used to play cricket together, Nirmal and I. On the maidan, in the winter. Good old days. *(beat)* You've passed your test, Rani. I failed. I couldn't kill Craig. I killed an Indian instead.

RANI. A collaborator. Good riddance!

BISWAS. We must kill him. Craig. *(pompously)* Inspector General of Police, Bengal! He's been inciting riots, again. All over.

RANI. Between Hindus and Muslims?

BISWAS. Haan.

RANI. And like fools we—

BISWAS. First they partitioned Bengal. Soon, they'll slice up the entire country. And the country will bleed, like a carcass in a butcher's shop in Kidderpore.

Rani laughs.

Shh!

RANI. Sorry, Ram da.

BISWAS. Sometimes, I wonder who's worse—the angrez who oppress, or us who permit the oppression.

RANI. There's nothing they've done to us that we haven't allowed them to do.

BISWAS. Clever girl. *(beat)* You will smuggle ammunition from Calcutta to Chittagong.

RANI. Haan, the angrez will never suspect a woman. Where will I get the guns?

BISWAS. Chinatown. The opium dens. That's where they are. 9mm pistols. Dynamite. Rifles.

RANI. What's the ammunition for, Ram da?

BISWAS. Pahartali Club, Chittagong. You know it?

RANI. Haan.

BISWAS. The angrez go there. With their wives, children, servants.

RANI. No Indian is allowed inside, dada.

BISWAS. 'No dogs, no Indians.' Craig goes there.

RANI. Pahartali Club?

BISWAS. Haan.

RANI. And that's where we'll kill him?

BISWAS. Haan.

RANI. When?

BISWAS. Surya will decide.

RANI. Suyra Sen?

BISWAS. Masterda.

RANI. Masterda. I've heard so much —

BISWAS. You'll meet him. You'll go back to Chittagong. You'll meet our Masterda. He's waiting for you.

RANI. *(beat)* I admire you, dada. More than you'll ever know. We admire you. All of us who are part of the revolution, all the women at the Chatri Sangha. You have shown us the way. Be fearless, be —

BISWAS. *(interrupting)* I am a terrorist, aren't I? *(beat)* 'Our mother's eyes are filled with tears. Her voice is broken and sad. A thousand wrongs have been heaped on her head. She calls, 'Which son of mine shall fight for her mother's honour?'

RANI. And what about her daughters?

BISWAS. What?

RANI. Every week, the people of Calcutta go to the Kali temple and make offerings to the mother goddess. They worship her, all these men, and yet, they see us — women who live with them, women who are their sisters, wives, mothers — they see *us* as... weak? Was the Rani of Jhansi weak? Were the Rajput princesses weak? They fought the British on horseback, dada! They killed with swords!

BISWAS. Calm, Rani, calm. All our ancient books plead for calm.

RANI. I studied philosophy for three years in college, dada. In this city. Words written by men. Locke, Hume, Kant, Plato. Being, doing, seeing. At the end of my studies, I realised I'd wasted my time.

BISWAS. What are you trying to say?

RANI. *(beat)* I was with my mother. When she gave birth. To Santosh, my little brother. In the little room of the house, beside the kitchen, overlooking the mango trees. Father wasn't around. No man was. I held onto my mother's right arm. Each time she cried, as Santosh lunged towards life, I felt Maa would die. Her insides would spill out. Maa said she felt like the flesh of her womb was being cut open with a knife. Blood everywhere. When Santosh arrived, I saw Maa change. The moment before, she was dying with pain, a second later, she took Santosh in her arms, in her love. *(beat)*. Nothing worth knowing in life comes from the mind, dada. Nothing.

BISWAS. *Nothing? Nothing will come of—*

RANI. Nothing. *(beat)* Sometimes I wish I'd never read Shakespeare. Never learnt the language. Never read a word of it.

BISWAS. Then burn the books.

RANI. What?

BISWAS. Burn Shakespeare. Burn all these English books. *(beat)* The first bomb I made, you know what I did? I collected all my English books in a bag, and took it, the bag, to a clearing in a field of jute, outside the city. I fixed the timer of the bomb, gave it five minutes, placed it inside the bag, and ran, ran through that field of jute, as if I had wild dogs snapping at my heels. I found the shade of a banyan tree, and I watched those books explode, the pages all ashed and black and scattered all over the bright yellow sky, like the feathers of a crow. And I felt free Rani, I felt free. *(beat)* It's time.

RANI. Is there a way?

BISWAS. What?

RANI. To get you out of here.

BISWAS. Shhh — they're watching.

RANI. Don't care.

BISWAS. Calm, Rani, calm.

RANI. You're not scared?

BISWAS. Na.

RANI. The noose, death?

BISWAS. I can't be afraid, Rani. *(beat)* I believe, Rani. I believe in —

Chorus enters as a guard.

CHORUS. Ki hocche? Chalo!

BISWAS. *(to the guard)* 'I will give my life for my motherland. You are to threaten us with death? Death has no terror for us.'

CHORUS. Haan, good, good. *(to Rani)* Chalo.

Rani and Biswas stare at each other. For the first time, their hands reach out and touch. They exit.

ACT I | SCENE 4

CHORUS. A woman and a man in jail, in the 1930s, in Calcutta. Forty-five years later, in 1975, we have another woman and another man in another jail, in the same city! The jail of marriage, the dungeon of family life, the prison bars of pregnancy!

Chorus becomes Durga, who is visibly pregnant and watching television. Shyamal enters.

SHYAMAL. Can't believe you watch that crap!

DURGA. Shhh!

SHYAMAL. We've got to talk.

DURGA. Shhh!

SHYAMAL. Durga, what's wrong with you?

DURGA. Not now! Can't you see, he's —

SHYAMAL. Give me a break!

DURGA. C'mon, even *you* like Amitabh Bachchan.

SHYAMAL. God help us if this is the best we can do.

DURGA. Ya, I forgot, Amitabh's not white enough for you, na?

SHYAMAL. Turn that bloody noise down.

DURGA. *(playing)* No I bloody won't.

SHYAMAL. If you won't, I bloody will.

DURGA. Don't you bloody dare.

SHYAMAL. Enough of this.

Shyamal goes and switches off the television set.

DURGA. I can't believe you...that's the scene where —

SHYAMAL. We don't have any money, Durga! Here you are... watching your stupid Bombay films —

DURGA. What do you mean?

SHYAMAL. I've done some calculations.

DURGA. And?

SHYAMAL. We can't live on five thousand rupees a month.

DURGA. Combined? You and me?

SHYAMAL. Yes.

DURGA. Then let Bahadur go. We don't need him. He spends all his time drinking anyway.

SHYAMAL. I need him.

DURGA. As your slave? Do this, do that.

SHYAMAL. I will not let him go, Durga.

DURGA. I don't understand you, what do you —

SHYAMAL. Keep your voice down, Durga!

DURGA. I'm not the one shouting!

SHYAMAL. Calm, calm, too much noise, I need calm.

DURGA. *(teasing him)* You're losing it, eh?

SHYAMAL. Shut up!

DURGA. Quiet! The baby —

SHYAMAL. Of course, he hears everything —

DURGA. Of course he does, ask the doctor —

SHYAMAL. The doctor's a quack —

DURGA. What? Quack? *(beat)* Sit down.

SHYAMAL. No.

DURGA. Why? Tense?

SHYAMAL. Yes.

DURGA. Don't be.

SHYAMAL. Easy for you to say.

DURGA. We have each other.

SHYAMAL. Enough with the melodrama. You've been watching too many films, you know... all this... emotional crap! Can't we have a rational conversation sometime? *(beat)* We're going to have a child, Durga.

DURGA. And?

SHYAMAL. We can't afford it. We can't bring up a family on five thousand rupees.

DURGA. What are you saying?

SHYAMAL. How will we — there's not enough to —

DURGA. *(interrupting)* You want me to kill it?

SHYAMAL. I didn't say that!

DURGA. I know how your mind works, Shyamal.

SHYAMAL. Don't flatter yourself.

DURGA. I don't. You do. I can't believe you — you really want me to get rid of it?

SHYAMAL. No.

DURGA. It's too late anyway. You've missed your chance.

Suddenly, the phone — an old rotary dial black phone — rings, and scares Durga.

Baap re baap!

Shyamal picks up the phone.

SHYAMAL. Hello. *(beat)* Yes, tell me, Pradip. Hmm? Uh-huh. Okay. Yes, rehearsals this evening, I know. Had a day off at the office today. Pleasures of working in the public sector. Haha! Durga's fine, yaar, thanks. Getting bigger by the day! Tell me, what's — *(beat)* What do you mean? *(beat)* How — no that doesn't make sense, you can't — yes yes, I know it's an important show, but I've been working on this part for years, you know that. *(beat)* And so what if some idiot at the Statesman thinks I'm — *(beat)* So who — who is it then? Come off it, Pradip, you can't be — I mean, you can't — and why you couldn't say all this to me in person? Face to face. Man to man. Tell me, you — always hiding, aren't you, Pradip? If Ian asks you to lick his shoe, you'll bloody do it, na? *(beat)* Oh yes, don't worry, I understand. I damn well understand. And no, I'm not going to play another role, thank you very fucking much!

Shyamal slams the phone down.

DURGA. What happened, Shyamal?

SHYAMAL. Nothing.

DURGA. Tell me.

SHYAMAL. They've found someone else. Some bloody Anglo-Indian. To play Richard.

DURGA. How could they? It's your role. You've played it. You know it. What does this — what does he have that you —

SHYAMAL. *(interrupting)* White skin. And all these bloody Europeans living in this city still prefer one of their own — and so do their Indian lackeys. The British left, but their ghosts still live on in Calcutta.

DURGA. I've always said that. Didn't think I'd hear these words from your mouth—

SHYAMAL. What's the point of it all?

DURGA. What, Shyamal?

Pause.

SHYAMAL. I loved my school teachers. Father Cox, Father Peter. Good men, Durga. I owe them everything. *(beat)* What's the point? My dreams of England. Shakespeare, cricket, fair play. *(beat)* I love the English language more than life itself, Durga. And all I ever get is rejection.

DURGA. Now, who's being melodramatic, Shyamal?

SHYAMAL. You know the study of English literature was first introduced in Calcutta, not in England?

DURGA. To civilise the natives?

SHYAMAL. For people like me. *(beat)* You see the streets outside, no? *(beat, then to himself)* Dante's inferno. If Dante had seen Calcutta, he wouldn't have bothered writing ever again. *(beat)* The whole city's gone to the dogs, people are being shot on the streets, there are no jobs, and here I am talking about English literature! We don't even have electricity for half the day—

DURGA. We're wasting ourselves in this city, Shyamal. If there's no future here, why stay?

SHYAMAL. *(almost to himself)* Calcutta, capital of the Raj. Glory of the East. What Bengal thinks today, India thinks tomorrow!

DURGA. *(firmly)* Past is past, Shyamal. *(beat)* What about Shesha, Alfred, Tommy — they've all left this place. They've all —

SHYAMAL. *(overlaps)* Bombay. Shesha says there are jobs, many jobs, in Bombay. Big banks. Foreign money —

DURGA. We have friends there. We could even stay with them for the first few months. Change is good. And I'm with you. We're with you.

SHYAMAL. Always?

DURGA. Always.

SHYAMAL. I'm not sure, I — *(beat)* It's a different world, there. Money, money, money. That's what they all say. No security, no free time to read, to act in plays. How will we survive? How will I —

DURGA. You will. We will. We're having a child, Shyamal. Life changes.

Shyamal pours himself a whiskey. He and Durga sit next to each other. They rest their heads together. Durga rubs her belly.

SHYAMAL. Do you even know me, Durga?

DURGA. What? *(beat)* Touch it.

Shyamal runs his hand over her belly, almost hesitating.

You don't even want to touch it—

SHYAMAL. It's beautiful.

DURGA. Liar. Why are you drinking so much?

SHYAMAL. I want to see the world through an alcoholic haze!

(pause)

I hardly drink—

DURGA. That's what they all say.

SHYAMAL. Who?

DURGA. And do you—

SHYAMAL. What?

DURGA. Nothing.

SHYAMAL. Tell me.

DURGA. Do you know what I want, Shyamal?

SHYAMAL. What are you saying?

DURGA. Do you think I want to spend the rest of my life teaching poor children how to read and write?

SHYAMAL. What do you want then?

DURGA. I don't know.

SHYAMAL. Then?

DURGA. We could have a better life. All three of us. I think you need to talk to Shesha.

SHYAMAL. Hmm?

DURGA. Call Shesha. Bombay.

SHYAMAL. Yes.

DURGA. Pick up the phone.

SHYAMAL. What?

DURGA. Pick up the phone!

SHYAMAL. Now?

DURGA. No, next year!

Shyamal gets up and goes to the phone, picks it up, turns the dial, sips his whiskey, fiddles with the receiver, slams it down again.

DURGA. What's the matter?

SHYAMAL. Not working.

DURGA. Phone?

SHYAMAL. No, my head!

DURGA. I'd believe that.

SHYAMAL. The phone, Durga, the phone!

DURGA. Again?

SHYAMAL. Yes, again. *(beat)* Nothing ever works in this shithole city.

ACT I | SCENE 5

CHORUS. It's 1976 and Durga and Shyamal and their unborn child decide to move to Bombay. Meanwhile, back in the roaring 30s, Rani, our intrepid heroine, has moved to Chittagong. She's smuggled arms and ammunition on the local trains, slept alongside cattle, slipped through entry posts and borders! And now, after many trips back and forth, she finds herself in Chittagong with her old friend, Kalpana Dutta!

Chorus becomes Kalpana. Rani and Kalpana in a room, preparing food.

RANI. How long?

KALPANA. What?

RANI. You and me?

KALPANA. Long time, Rani. You remember — our schooldays —

RANI. We wanted to be scientists.

KALPANA. Haan, imagine.

RANI. And here we are...

KALPANA. Cooking.

RANI. Fighting for our country!

KALPANA. Feeding the men who are fighting for the country.

RANI. It's all part of the cause, Kalpana.

KALPANA. Is it? I don't know why we have to prepare the food! Every day. Look at this—my hands are numb from all this... this—rice, daal, fish nonsense. This is still our lot, Rani.

RANI. How can you say that, Kalpana? We've transported guns. We've learnt to make bombs—

KALPANA. *(interrupting)* You know how hard it is to enter the world of men?

RANI. We're here now—

KALPANA. Even the best of them...I still think...still feel...in their hearts, they—

RANI. Look down on us?

KALPANA. Haan.

RANI. If they do, I'll chop their heads off!

KALPANA. Like the Rani of Jhansi!

RANI. Chopping off British heads on horseback!

KALPANA. Baap re baap, such a tiger, my Rani!

RANI. We will fight with our brothers—

KALPANA. We are, we will—

RANI. We can. We will. We are modern Indian woman. We shall no longer lag behind our brothers. If they work in offices, so shall we. If they study at universities, so shall we. If they fire guns, so shall we—

KALPANA. Save this for your speeches, Rani.

RANI. I'm not lying, Kalpana. If I've done it, so shall every Indian woman—

KALPANA. If they don't set her on fire. Or trade her like cattle. Or ask her to hide her face—*(beat)* Look at us, Rani. Look at what we're doing.

Pause.

RANI. How are your parents?

KALPANA. Fine.

RANI. What would they do if they—

KALPANA. Knew? That I'm fighting the angrez?

RANI. Haan.

KALPANA. Kill me.

RANI. I can't imagine your father hurting a fly.

KALPANA. When we were in school, I used to tell him that I wanted to become a revolutionary. All he said was—'study hard, grow up, and then do whatever you want.' Still, if he knew—*(beat)* Did you know my grandfather was given the title of Rai Bahadur?

RANI. Na!

KALPANA. Haan! For services to the Raj! I've shamed them, Rani! How dare I fight against the people who've saved our once great nation!

RANI. They really believe that?

KALPANA. Why wouldn't they? They make money off the British, na? They help throw Indians in jail, they tax them, sentence them. They are selling this land to the angrez. *(beat)* I hate my father.

RANI. Don't say that—

KALPANA. I can't believe he doesn't know the angrez will never treat us as equals!

RANI. Well, they've built some of our cities, our roads, our railways—

KALPANA. You as well, Rani?

RANI. It's not me. It's what people like your father say. And the sad thing is they're right. *(beat)* I'm sorry.

KALPANA. For what?

RANI. Na... I mean... it must be hard for you—

KALPANA. I used to be scared. Of my parents finding out. Of their shame. *(beat)* Let them find out. Let them learn their daughter will fight with every muscle in her bones to kick the angrez out of this country!

RANI. And what about you?

KALPANA. What do you mean?

RANI. How does it feel?

KALPANA. What?

RANI. To come from such a family? A family of —

KALPANA. Bootlickers?

Sudden, insistent knock on the door.

RANI. Who?

Kalpana goes to open the door. Sound of a man's voice outside. Rani, alone on stage. Kalpana re-enters. The two old friends stare at each other, silently.

RANI. What happened? Seen a ghost?

KALPANA. He wants to see you.

RANI. Who?

KALPANA. Surya Sen.

RANI. Masterda!

KALPANA. Masterda —

RANI. Now?

KALPANA. Soon. He's coming.

RANI. I can't believe—

KALPANA. Scared?

RANI. Why should I be scared of one of our own?

KALPANA. Because he's a man?

RANI. And I am a woman, Kalpana.

KALPANA. You're fidgeting, Rani—

RANI. *(interrupting)* I want to meet him, Kalpana! I can't wait any longer. The others will be there? Nirmal?

KALPANA. Haan.

RANI. Thank god!

KALPANA. What's so special about Nirmal?

RANI. Don't know what you mean.

KALPANA. Nirmal, O Nirmal!

RANI. Kalpana! Enough!

KALPANA. Baap re baap, so it's true?

RANI. What?

KALPANA. What they say about Nirmal. And you.

RANI. What! Who?

KALPANA. Won't tell.

RANI. What's he like?

KALPANA. Who?

RANI. Surya Sen. Masterda.

KALPANA. Quiet, shy almost, I think. A bit like you, Rani.

RANI. I'm not shy.

KALPANA. He's short. Nothing special in looks. A strange man. A quiet man. And we all look up to him. And he's... *(beat)* No one cares more, and yet, sometimes... I almost feel like he's... like he's not there. You'll see.

RANI. What if he doesn't like me?

KALPANA. Baap re baap, Rani, I think you should run away with Nirmal da, get married, have children, raise them together, live happily ever after.

RANI. As if he'd ever leave.

KALPANA. So you've thought about it?

RANI. What?

KALPANA. Running away.

RANI. Na.

KALPANA. You have!

RANI. Na!

KALPANA. Liar.

RANI. And Masterda? Does he know?

KALPANA. What?

RANI. About your family?

KALPANA. *(in a panic)* Na!

RANI. Why not? You should tell him.

KALPANA. If you dare tell him anything, I'll—

RANI. How far will you go?

KALPANA. For what?

RANI. To protect your secret?

KALPANA. You're questioning *me*, Rani? When I'm the one who—

RANI. We can't tolerate divided loyalties. How do I know you won't betray us?

KALPANA. *Us*, she says!

RANI. I'll tell him.

KALPANA. No you won't.

RANI. I will.

KALPANA. Na!

Kalpana lunges for Rani, pulls her by the hair. They play-fight like children.

RANI. Let me go! Let me —

The continue fighting. They stop, they pant, they laugh.

KALPANA. In this world of men, we need to be together. Always. If one of us falls, we all fall.

RANI. Ei je! Now you're the one with the big words, Kalpana!

KALPANA. Stop being so smart, Rani! *(beat)* It's time. He'll be here soon. *(beat)*You're ready, Rani. I never doubted you.

RANI. Will he like me?

KALPANA. *(laughing)* Come here, my child!

Rani rests her head on Kalpana. Pause.

You won't tell him, will you?

RANI. What?

KALPANA. Nothing.

RANI. Tell —

KALPANA. Na, just... you won't tell him about my family? Will you?

Rani smiles, doesn't say anything. She touches Kalpana on her shoulder, runs her fingers through her hair. The sound of knocking, and a man coughing.

ACT I | SCENE 6

Dhalgat village, east of Chittagong. Rani and Nirmal Sen in a room.

RANI. Won't you come?

NIRMAL. Na.

RANI. Please come.

NIRMAL. Na, Rani, you go, I'll be here.

RANI. Why?

NIRMAL. Not feeling — *(beat)* He's waiting for you. Stop behaving like a little girl, now. I'm not feeling well.

RANI. Let me take care of you.

NIRMAL. Take care of yourself and I'll be happy.

RANI. He scares me.

NIRMAL. Who? Surya?

RANI. Haan.

NIRMAL. Why? You can't be serious, he's a—

RANI. Don't know, I'm... *(beat)* It's just that, he's so... he makes me shy!

NIRMAL. You *are* shy, Rani!

RANI. I'm not!

NIRMAL. Then what's the problem?

Nirmal clutches his stomach suddenly and moans.

RANI. What happened?

NIRMAL. Ooof! Must be the eggs this afternoon!

RANI. Digestion problems?

NIRMAL. Shitting problems.

RANI. Again?

NIRMAL. Haan!

RANI. Is it hard?

NIRMAL. Haan.

RANI. Very?

NIRMAL. Haan!

RANI. *(goes to fetch a bottle)* Here, take some pudin hara.

NIRMAL. My angel! Ooof, you can recognize a Bengali by his smelly farts!

RANI. And his need to talk about it.

NIRMAL. Why not? Shitting is the most philosophical moment of the day. When I sit on my haunches — in the fields, or in the city, doesn't matter — I come face to face with reality. Mortality. All this being, doing, seeing you studied in Calcutta, Rani —

RANI. *(overlapping)* Rubbish!

NIRMAL. *(overlapping)* It all comes to nothing when we're face to face, every morning, with the sight and smell of our own shit. We look down at it, it stares back up at us and says — 'see see babumoshai, look closely, inhale deeply, after all the fighting's done, this is what you really are, a massive pile of manure!' This, dear Rani, is why Bengalis, the poets and painters and scientists of this land, talk endlessly about the smell and texture of their own shit.

RANI. Vah vah, Nirmal Da, such inspiring words, from the mouth of a revolutionary!

NIRMAL. All hail Bengal's love of shit! Aamar sonar bangla, glory to golden Bengal, bande materam, jai hind!

Nirmal suddenly clutches his stomach and wails.

Ooof! Aar pachchi na! My god, what I'd give for a good —

He wails.

RANI. I can't believe you, Nirmal! Eat eat eat! All the time! Talk about the next meal while eating the last. Then, spend the rest of the night in —

NIRMAL. And to think there are millions in this country that are starving!

RANI. *(giving Nirmal a dose of the Ayurvedic medicine)* Well, you're fighting for them. Here, there, like a good boy. Good, haan, good. You'll be up and running in an hour, I promise you.

NIRMAL. Promise me freedom, Rani!

RANI. Ei Je! That too shall come —

NIRMAL. One day!

RANI. One day!

NIRMAL. *(holding the bottle of medicine)* Till then, we have Pudin Hara! Made from pudina satva, mint leaves, providing instant and effective relief from indigestion, stomach pain and —

RANI & NIRMAL. *(together)* Gas!

They laugh. The sound of voices downstairs, as if sitting down to a meal.

NIRMAL. I miss you when you're not around.

RANI. What?

NIRMAL. I miss you when —

RANI. *(interrupting)* Don't say that —

NIRMAL. Why? It's true. Don't you?

RANI. Haan.

NIRMAL. Then?

RANI. I'm scared.

NIRMAL. Of what?

RANI. Don't know.

NIRMAL. *(beat)* Wouldn't it be nice?

RANI. What?

NIRMAL. To go somewhere. Just you and me—

Rani starts to laugh.

You find this funny?

RANI. Na. Just that—

NIRMAL. It's a dream Rani. You have to dream.

RANI. Like our dream of freedom?

NIRMAL. Haan.

RANI. No different?

NIRMAL. Na.

RANI. Promise?

NIRMAL. Haan.

RANI. One day?

NIRMAL. One day.

RANI. Where? Where will we go?

NIRMAL. You tell me.

RANI. Bombay?

NIRMAL. Why?

RANI. The city by the sea.

NIRMAL. We have the sea here in Chittagong, Rani. Why go anywhere else?

RANI. I'm dreaming, Nirmal, just—

NIRMAL. What, Rani?

RANI. Nothing! It's just—I feel so full of dreams I want to cry!

NIRMAL. Come here, sweet child.

Rani rests her head on Nirmal's shoulder. Nirmal reaches out, pulls out a big book.

RANI. Shakespeare?

NIRMAL. A Bengali's great love. Along with the smell of his own shit. *(beat)* For you.

RANI. Why?

NIRMAL. Can't read it anymore. Keep it.

RANI. Ram da said we should burn all our English books.

NIRMAL. Did he? We should. Forget all about the English language. Like a bad dream. *(beat)* What?

RANI. Nothing. How's the stomach?

NIRMAL. Hmm?

RANI. Stomach?

NIRMAL. Arre, all hail pudin hara!

RANI. Come na, Nirmal.

NIRMAL. Where?

RANI. Downstairs.

NIRMAL. Na. Let me rest.

RANI. I don't know what to say to him.

NIRMAL. Don't be silly, Rani. You've seen Surya. He won't say a word.

RANI. That's my point! He's so... I don't know... he's never said anything to me. I feel like he's watching me all the time. Judging me. Waiting to see if I'll break, if I'll run away. And I... I don't know what to say to him. Come, Nirmal, I want you to —

NIRMAL. *(interrupting)* Shhh! You hear that?

RANI. What?

NIRMAL. Listen! What's that?

RANI. The sound of the wind in the —

NIRMAL. Shhh! Na... footsteps.

RANI. Sure?

NIRMAL. Listen!

RANI. Can't hear —

NIRMAL. Shhh!

Sound of wind blowing through trees outside, voices downstairs.

Hear anything?

RANI. I hear... I hear... the sound of your stomach growling!

Suddenly, the sound of gunfire. Rani screams.

NIRMAL. Shhh! You're a warrior now, Rani. Go!

RANI. Where?

NIRMAL. To Surya, go!

Rani rushes downstage, Shakespeare in hand, to Surya Sen, dressed in a kurta and trousers. Nirmal is shot. Rani rushes towards Nirmal, but Surya pulls her back, and tries dragging her away. We see Nirmal gesticulating wildly, communicating that she must go with Surya, that he'll stay back and keep shooting. Nirmal is shot again. Rani wails. Surya drags her away.

ACT I | SCENE 7

CHORUS. That was pretty hairy, wasn't it! A gunfight in Dhalghat! Nirmal dies, and Rani escapes. That's just the way the story goes. Nirmal and Rani, Rani and Nirmal! Did Nirmal sacrifice himself for her? What do you think? Meanwhile, flash forward to the 1970s, and after years of ploughing through amateur dramatics and bad accounting in Calcutta, Shyamal and his young family are in Bombay, the city by the sea. Yes yes, Bombay, India's dazzling whore, monstrous pimp, all warts and all! Bombay, not Mumbai! Ground zero for the Anglicised Indian!

Chorus becomes Durga. Next to her, baby Ananda in a pram. Durga pushes the pram from time to time, looks at him lovingly. Shyamal speaks on the phone, while fixing a whiskey.

SHYAMAL. *(phone)* Okay, I know, ya. Okay. Ya, I'll be seeing the Japs tomorrow, yaar. They're crazy. Drink like mad. Even I have a hard time keeping up with them. *(beat)* No no, I want the car ready at 8pm, tomorrow, ya? We've got a table booked at The Golden Dragon. Followed by drinks at the Sea Lounge, hmm? Great great— *(beat)* I'll be there when I'm there. Fashionably late and all yaar. *(beat)* Sell them the whole spiel, Bombay's booming and all. This is the place to invest. Bang for your buck. Take them straight to town. Show them Marine Drive, they'll be impressed, ya? Thanks Nakul. Great, see you then, see you tomorrow. Bye.

Beat, then Shyamal slams the phone down.

DURGA. What's wrong with you?

SHYAMAL. Hmm?

DURGA. The baby's asleep—

SHYAMAL. So?

DURGA. Don't slam the phone down like that! The baby —

SHYAMAL. Enough with the baby! *(beat)* Sorry.

DURGA. What happened?

SHYAMAL. Hmm?

DURGA. Why so serious and all?

SHYAMAL. 'Bang for your buck.' Can't believe the words I use these
    days. These boys in the bank, like Nakul, they're very, you know,
    I guess, influenced by America.

DURGA. The Brits left, and now the Americans are moving in.

SHYAMAL. *(blankly)* Real estate prices in Bombay are nudging those
    of New York, London, Tokyo, says Nakul. Altamount Road, Cuffe
    Parade, Malabar Hill, those areas of the city. But the economy still
    needs to open up, he says. We still have foreign exchange controls.
    Can't take money out of the country if you go abroad. Takes years
    to get a phone installed. Can't buy foreign goods without paying
    tax. Can't do this, can't do that, he says. Our leaders are stuck in
    the past. Time for change, Nakul says.

Baby Ananda wails in the pram.

God, Durga, can't you keep him quiet!?

DURGA. You can do it yourself. Babies cry—

SHYAMAL. I'm far too busy with the bank and you know it!

DURGA. So am I.

SHYAMAL. Doing what?

DURGA. Really now, do we need this?

SHYAMAL. *(beat)* I used recite poetry. Now, I recite bank balances.

DURGA. Oh god, Shyamal, not that again.

SHYAMAL. It's all your fault.

DURGA. What? Do you really —

SHYAMAL. *(interrupting)* I was happy in Calcutta. Doing my plays. Working in the public sector. Cushy job —

DURGA. Stop, I can't deal with your moaning anymore —

SHYAMAL. *(overlapping)* But no, you didn't want that. You wanted me to move to Bombay, make money, so you could tell your family, 'Look, look, my husband's made a success of himself!' Isn't that what you wanted?

DURGA. No one forced you into anything. Your life is your own. If you want to be a failure, go ahead, be my guest —

SHYAMAL. *(overlapping)* How dare you?

DURGA. *(overlapping)* I certainly won't be around. We won't —

SHYAMAL. Don't you even care?

DURGA. Have some sympathy, Shyamal. How many times do I have to listen to the same thing, haan? How many times? Every day, same thing. I've got a child to look after. I can't take care of you as well. I'm exhausted —

SHYAMAL. My life's a failure.

DURGA. You're lucky, Shyamal. You're making good money for the first time in your life. You have me, you have your son, be grateful —

SHYAMAL. I could've been an actor. A teacher. A university professor —

DURGA. Have you lost your mind? Professors get paid peanuts in this country —

SHYAMAL. Anything but a bloody banker!

DURGA. Enough, Shyamal, I can't take this! Can't you see? I need your help —

Baby Ananda cries again.

SHYAMAL. We don't fuck anymore.

DURGA. What? I need to change him. Turn the geyser on. Get me some warm water. Some cotton.

SHYAMAL. I can't do all this. Where's Bahadur?

DURGA. How should I know? Lying drunk somewhere. And I certainly don't want him touching Ananda.

Baby Ananda cries again.

SHYAMAL. I've had enough! You're all going to drive me mad! I need a drink —

DURGA. You and Bahadur make a great pair. Master and servant. I don't know who takes care of whom.

SHYAMAL. What did you say?

DURGA. You drink too much, Shyamal. I've been telling you for years —

SHYAMAL. Enough!

DURGA. I'm sorry you're unhappy —

Baby Ananda cries again.

SHYAMAL. If that boy was older, I'd hammer him into shape!

DURGA. Ananda, please. *(beat)* He's a baby, Shyamal. Please don't talk like that.

SHYAMAL. And what if I do?

DURGA. I'll leave you.

SHYAMAL. I'd like to see that.

DURGA. Be careful of what you wish for.

SHYAMAL. None of that namby-pamby shit in this house. When I was growing up, the cane and the belt were used to keep me in shape. *(laughs, then halts abruptly).* Nothing wrong with a bit of discipline, nothing wrong—

DURGA. He's a baby, Shyamal.

SHYAMAL. I don't care.

DURGA. You raise your voice at me again—you insult me again—*(beat)* I'll leave you, I promise!

Baby Ananda cries again.

SHYAMAL. Where will you go? Answer me. Where?

DURGA. Don't worry about me.

SHYAMAL. I always worry about you.

DURGA. I have places to go.

SHYAMAL. Do you now?

DURGA. Stop drinking so much. The baby will end being as unhappy as you—

SHYAMAL. Quiet!

Baby Ananda cries again.

DURGA. If we lived in another country, you know, your precious England, I certainly would've left you!

SHYAMAL. Get out!

DURGA. Your son needs you, Shyamal.

SHYAMAL. Get out!

DURGA. Don't you ever talk to me like that again!

Shyamal throws his whiskey glass on the floor. It shatters. Baby Ananda starts howling, a long, continuous howl. Durga is shocked and still.

SHYAMAL. Stop this wailing, Durga! Stop! Stop him, I can't take it anymore! Enough! Stop now. Stop—

Shyamal pushes the pram, which slides to the other end of the stage. The howling continues.

DURGA. *(shocked)* Who are you?

SHYAMAL. Your lord and master.

DURGA. Monster!

SHYAMAL. Work is driving me mad, Durga. I'm working for you, for him, for—

DURGA. *(interrupting)* I'm leaving. We're leaving. I can't spend the rest of my life with an unhappy man. Sorry babu, don't listen to Mummy. Or Daddy. *(beat)* Goodbye, Shyamal.

Durga picks up baby Ananda and starts to leave.
I'll be back for my things—

Shyamal tries desperately to stop them.

SHYAMAL. Please!

DURGA. Don't touch me!

SHYAMAL. You can't... I won't allow —

Durga and Shyamal struggle. Baby Ananda wails in Durga's arms.

I won't...!

Durga slaps Shyamal. Shock and awe. Pause.

DURGA. I enjoyed that.

Durga and baby Ananda leave. Shyamal is left alone on stage. Shyamal walks around the empty stage like a lost boy, stunned. Silence. The doorbell rings.

SHYAMAL. Durga!

Shyamal runs to opens the door. Bahadur enters.

BAHADUR. Sahib —

Shyamal hits Bahadur on the head. He falls to the floor.

BAHADUR. *(scared)* Sahib!

Shyamal goes to kick him and stops at the last second. Turns around and gives a short, sharp wail.

BAHADUR. *(getting up)* Shobh thik aache, sahib?

SHYAMAL. *(composing himself)* What? Yes yes, everything's fine. Go, go —

Shyamal motions Bahadur to clean up the broken glass. Bahadur fetches a broom and starts sweeping, almost in slow motion. He keeps sweeping, in slow motion, till the end of the scene.

SHYAMAL. *(to himself) A*nd since I cannot prove a lover to entertain — (beat) I am determined to prove — *(beat)* a villain...and hate... — *(beat)* Shit, can't remember.

Bahadur sweeps away. On the opposite end of the stage, Rani enters, with a copy of Shakespeare's Complete Works.

SHYAMAL. But I that am not... shaped... sportive tricks... dogs bark...

Shyamal continues. Rani places Shakespeare on the ground. As Shyamal continues to recite the words, as Bahadur continues sweeping, Rani sets Shakespeare on fire. The book burns.

SHYAMAL. Is this — who am I?

ACT II

SCENE 1

Bombay 2017. Ruksana, Ananda and Yogesh: a continuation of Act I Scene I.

RUKSANA. *(continuing her story)* So, next afternoon, Thomas the Nigerian dealer's in Goa and I'm waiting for him, you know, and Thomas arrives, and he gets out of the cab and—

YOGESH. Mad gandu!

RUKSANA. He's all dressed up in a suit, a leopard stripe suit, I kid you not, and a black hat, and he's carrying a cane, man he's got a chutiya cane with him! Just picture it, ya? You have this big African guy in the middle of Goa dressed in a leopard suit, and he says—

YOGESH. *(in a mock deep voice)* 'If I'm coming to Goa, then I'm coming to party! Yeah!'

All three friends are laughing now. Ruksi sticks her hand out and the scene freezes.

RUKSANA. *(to audience)* Welcome back, ladies and gentlemen, mesdames et messieurs, aadmis and aurats, welcome back from the official pee break, yes! This is where it all started an hour ago. And now that your bladder's more relaxed, we can return to Bombay 2017. Shall we continue?

Ruksi/ Chorus claps, and the scene cuts back to laughter and action.

RUKSANA. You stole my line, you chooth, Yogi!

YOGESH. There are cops crawling all over the place like ants, but Thomas doesn't give two fucks—

RUKSANA. I couldn't have managed without him!

YOGESH. That nigger's a G!

ANANDA. *(beat)* You can't say that!

RUKSANA. He's joking yaar.

YOGESH. And who are you, brother? Mother Teresa?

ANANDA. Some shit you just don't say.

YOGESH. Vah! Of course, I agree master, thy will be done!

ANANDA. I just wish we'd stop being so racist—

YOGESH. This is India chooth, India, get it? And that's the last time you tell me what I can and can't say in my own pad, ya?

RUKSANA. Chill, yaar, Yogi.

YOGESH. I'm serious. No respect, haan? I'll say whatever I want, boss! This is not the UK! You want me to repeat myself, haan? Bloody Paki!

ANANDA. Relax.

YOGESH. Tell me, maderchod!

RUKSANA. Chill yaar, Yogi!

YOGESH. You want me to repeat myself?

ANANDA. No.

YOGESH. Coz I can't hear you bhenchod!

ANANDA. I'm sorry.

YOGESH. *(beat)* Bloody foreigner! Play with him and he starts apologizing like he's got rats in his pants! I'm messing with you, gandu!

Ruksi lights a smoke.

Gimme a drag, na!

RUKSANA. Get your own —

YOGESH. Give, na!

Ruksi gives Yogesh her cigarette. Yogesh puffs, inhales, exhales, blowing smoke rings.

YOGESH. *(Cyprus Hill)* 'Inhale, exhale, got an ounce in the mail!' That's better. And let me tell you something, boss. I take the auto to Juhu man. Every day. You know the spot where you turn into Juhu Tara, right? Next to Jamnabhai?

RUKSANA. He's been away for years, Yogi.

YOGESH. So he's forgotten everything, haan? *(beat)* Every morning in Juhu, there's this beggar who's got no legs, ya? And he's on this wooden plank, and he's pushing himself with the stumps of his hands. Part of the city's crazy scenery. Perfect for tourists like you.

RUKSANA. Cut it, yaar.

YOGESH. And if it's hot, he's bloody dying. He's wearing an old, tattered white shirt. He's got this gamcha on his head. Tiny gray shorts. His legs are like toothpicks. He sees me everyday. In the beginning, you feel bad and shit. You toss a few coins into this little stainless steel container of his. Sometimes, he just taps on the auto with his little stumps. The hands look like they've been chewed off by an animal. Like one of the wild dogs of Bombay has just ripped them off and carried them away in between his canines, ya? But our beggar's still got a smile on his face. And if it's hot, the driver takes the water he uses for his engine, opens the bottle for the beggar and pours it down his throat, like petrol. The poor soul drinks, still tapping on the auto with a stump, as if saying 'thank you, thank you bhaisaab'. Then he goes away, pushing himself, hustling through the crazy honking traffic. Sometimes, I just wanna scream at the sight of him. But what can you do? This is Bombay. It's the law of the jungle out there, bhai. Kill or be killed. Eat or be eaten. Jungle Raj, Ananda. You think after all this I have time for your silly political correctness?

ANANDA. You're just confusing things bhai.

YOGESH. Don't bloody 'bhai' me, okay? And you know what? None of these beggars wants our pity, ya? No matter how screwed up his life is, each one has his own movie running in his head.

RUKSANA. Or *her* head.

YOGESH. Movies with songs and dances, and each one thinks he's gonna be the king of Bombay. Even if he's got no hands. Get it?

ANANDA. *(beat)* Got it.

YOGESH. That's ma dog!

Pause.

RUKSANA. How does it feel?

ANANDA. Hmm?

RUKSANA. Being back?

ANANDA. Things are different. So much has changed. So much is still the same. The airport's like a spaceship from another planet. Makes Heathrow look so 20th century. But it's still surrounded by slums. Doesn't it bother you guys?

YOGESH. India's where it's at, boss. Get that in your head. Your Jaguar, your British Steel, all owned by a Bombay company, boss. That's some crazy shit. The Empire bites back!

ANANDA. Big talk Yogesh. A truly Bombay pastime. You're snorting too much blow.

YOGESH. The heads of Google, Microsoft, Pepsi. All pure desi man, all pure desi. Doesn't that make you proud?

RUKSANA. Ya, but what's that got to do with anything Yogesh? India still hasn't managed to cover the basics for half its people, and we're thumping our chests in front of the rest of the world cos we sent a tin can to Mars!

ANANDA. Listen, listen to your wife, chodu. Get that head out of your ass, Yogi!

YOGESH. The reality is that India doesn't care what you, or the rest of the world, thinks, Ananda. If there's one country we care about, it's China. That's the new game. We gotta catch up.

RUKSANA. When are you going back?

ANANDA. Haan?

RUKSANA. How long?

ANANDA. The funeral's in a few days. In Calcutta. Then, we'll see.

RUKSANA. You ready for it?

ANANDA. Hmm?

RUKSANA. You ready? Your dad? Seeing him like that? *(beat)* Sorry, yaar. It'll get better in a few years. The pain doesn't go away. You just learn to deal with it.

YOGESH. *(laughing)* Time is a great dealer!

ANANDA. No no, it's just like, I don't know, Ruksi. Sometimes I get this nasty feeling like I'm living the life he wanted for himself, you know? You remember him, na? Reading and reciting Shakespeare and all. What does all that have to do with us? With our reality? With all this? Maybe I went to England to please him. Maybe I just wanted to be the good Indian son. And now he's gone.

RUKSANA. Don't go back, yaar. For a person of your talent, the sky's the limit in India.

ANANDA. Been away too long, Ruksi. It's a bit late.

RUKSANA. It's never too late.

YOGESH. Screw this sentimental shit, you guys! Soon Ananda will be running round trees, singing songs and all!

ANANDA. You're right, Yogi, screw this shit. There's a part of me that hates India, hates this dirty, filthy, stinking shithole! Why do you think I stayed away so long? See through the big talk and hot air, and the whole country's a fucking mess —

YOGESH. D'you really think we need to hear this from *you*? Bloody foreigner —

ANANDA. I'm the foreigner? We're all bloody foreigners in India, man. You want to know what I'm writing about, Yogi? Well, listen. This country's still a bloody colony. For the last 70 years, we've been ruled by British-educated arselickers. Take the moment of our independence. We all know Nehru's speech, na? India's tryst with destiny, and all? What balls! Have you even realised that most Indians couldn't even understand a word of it? Cos it was in English, gandu. In bloody English! A language that most of this country still doesn't understand. (beat) I mean, here you are Yogi going all gaga and wah wah about India, but people like you are the last ones to talk about this place! I mean, look at you man? With your cocaine and drum and bass. You're obsessed with the West, but you wouldn't dare tell it like is, na? You won't even admit it to yourself. You're a fraud boss.

YOGESH. Just because I listen to Dn'B and snort cola doesn't make me a traitor, chooth. And English is my language.

RUKSANA. We are who we are, Ananda. Just because we speak

English doesn't make us oppressors, you know?

YOGESH. Ya, and anyway, it's all changing, bro.

ANANDA. What?

YOGESH. Today's India is ripe, full of juice, and ready to explode! And today's India doesn't speak in English, boss. And that's what makes people like you insecure. People like you, English-educated types, you're just passing away into history. Like your dad. Passed away into history! Puff! Just like that! Gone! No more Shakespeare! Now, you tell me, who's the fucking fraud?

Silence.

RUKSANA. Yogi, what's wrong with you?

YOGESH. I'm not the one who started talking about his dad—

ANANDA. How fucking dare you—

YOGESH. Take a chill pill, Ananda. Here, I'll cut another line—

Suddenly, Ananda lunges at Yogi. A scuffle ensues. Ruksi tries to break them up. Ananda tries to land a punch, slips, falls on the floor.

RUKSANA. *(shouting)* What's wrong with you guys! I think the coke's gone to your brain, Yogi!

ANANDA. He's dead, Yogi. He's dead. My dad's dead. He died of a heart attack! On his own!

Ananda is on the verge of breaking down. Ruksi sits beside him, takes him in her arms.

RUKSANA. Sorry Ananda, I know it's—

YOGESH. Sorry yaar, I didn't—

ANANDA. I should've been there. These last years. He was on his own. I should've—

RUKSANA. *(claps)* Chalo husband, proud of yourself?

YOGESH. Arre vah, Ananda, such a sensitive flower! This is what living in England has done to you? Chal, let's go grab a drink! There's a dubstep night happening in Worli!

RUKSANA. Don't listen to him, Ananda. It's all bigtalk. 'New India', my ass! If I could, I'd be out of this place tomorrow.

YOGESH. Speak for yourself, Ruksi.

RUKSANA. It sucks being a woman here. Take me back to England with you, Ananda.

Silence.

YOGESH. So who's cutting another line, man? Ruksi? Ananda? *(beat)* C'mon guys, this place feels like a fucking funeral!

ANANDA. Get lost, Yogi!

YOGESH. Don't know about you, but I'm ready to bloody party, Bombay ssshtyle!

Yogesh cuts a line.

ACT II | SCENE 2

CHORUS. Yes, ladies and gents, as the English-speaking stooges in today's Bombay drown in a hail of snow-white, high-grade cocaine, let's return to the world that Ananda has spent years reading about in England. Yes, yes, the supreme irony — in the heart of Empire, Ananda learns the history of revolt against that very Empire! Strange, na? Here we are, back in Chittagong, September 1932. Our heroine, Rani, has finally met Surya Sen, the leader of the Bengal revolutionaries. Sen has been been in hiding for years, on the run from the angrez. And to set the scene, dear people, to create the illusion of Bengal in the 1930s, we have the sounds of a Jatra troupe performing in the distance *(with each example, a fresh new sound emerges)*. Listen! A fruit-seller, koels, vegetable vendors, the azaan of the neighbourhood mosque! The full exotic shebang, you see!

Rani and Surya Sen in a room with a window and a chair. Sen is dressed as a conservative Muslim. During the scene, he slowly removes his beard, makeup, skullcap etc.

RANI. It's getting damp.

SEN. Hmm?

RANI. Getting damp.

SEN. The rain. It's cold.

Pause.

SEN. *(together)* You want to —

RANI. *(together)* How have you—

They laugh.

SEN. You first.

RANI. Na dada, you. You're older.

SEN. I didn't know you were so — *(beat)* I don't understand you, Rani. Sometimes so shy, and sometimes so—I don't know—how to—

RANI. You don't have to.

SEN. What?

RANI. Define me.

SEN. You confuse me. I'm still not sure about you. Should I trust you?

RANI. How can you even say that to me? I've given myself to the cause. Ever since Calcutta. I met Ramkrishna da in jail. I've transported ammunition all the way here. Made bombs. Trained in the martial arts. Learned to fire a gun. Anything you can do, I can do. And I have no fear, dada. Of anything. Or anyone. You know that. In your heart, you know I—

SEN. I know, I know. I'm sorry, I—

RANI. Don't play games, dada.

SEN. Lower your voice, Rani.

RANI. I don't have time for games.

SEN. You blame me for Nirmal?

RANI. No dada, how could —

SEN. You do. I can see it in your eyes — I couldn't do anything.

RANI. I never blamed you dada.

SEN. He was my best friend, Rani. Ever since he went away, I feel as if I've lost my arms, my eyes, my — *(beat)* Sometimes I see him in front of me. Or I hear his voice — 'Surya! Chalo, I smell the blood of an Englishman!' *(laughs)* Sometimes, at night, I wonder if... that night —

RANI. It's over, dada. He's gone. Have you seen Kalpana?

SEN. Strange, raining this time of the year, na? *(beat)* She's under house arrest. I'm in touch with her. You'll see her soon.

RANI. Will I?

SEN. Haan.

RANI. Why don't you sit down?

SEN. Hmm?

RANI. Sit.

Surya removes his skullcap, sits on a chair.

How have you been? None of us know where you are half the time.

SEN. Tired, Rani, tired. Of hiding in my own country. All dressed up as someone I'm not. Tired of wandering, Rani.

RANI. Aren't we all?

SEN. What? *(beat)* One day, if you're ever hunted by the British, you will have to disguise yourself too.

RANI. If only, dada, if only. I dream about that day. I'll do anything to be hunted by them. I'll wear their fear, and my rage, like a badge, I promise you.

SEN. Your rage will be your honour, Rani.

RANI. Will it? When? How? All I've been doing these past months is waiting, waiting.

SEN. Is it right to kill innocents, Rani?

RANI. Hmm? *(beat)* They have slaughtered us. Why should we be scared of killing their wives and children?

SEN. Something doesn't feel right. *(beat)* Look at me? A tired man, on the run, scared.

RANI. If you're scared, let me take over.

SEN. Quiet! *(beat)* The sahib is the new caste. The fairest of them all. 'No dogs, no Indians,' he tells us. In our own land.

RANI. And we speak their language, study it, like fools. Admire their ways. Their clothes, their dress, their talk. *(beat)* I remember the Bengalis of North Calcutta, aping every English custom they saw on Park Street, on their days out in white town. Laughing with their fat children. Speaking only English. Mocking their fellow Indians who couldn't speak it. Spitting on the poor. Making the sahib rich. Selling this land to him. These are the Indians the people of this country should fear. After the sahib leaves, his slaves will control India. Who are we really fighting for, Masterda?

SEN. *(abruptly)* You will lead the attack, Rani.

Pause.

RANI. *(shock)* What did you say?

SEN. Pahartali Club. Craig.

RANI. *(shock)* When?

SEN. This month. The night of the 23rd.

RANI. There's not much time —

SEN. You can refuse —

RANI. How can you say that? I can't believe this — I didn't think you'd — I don't know what to —

SEN. You will have to kill, Rani. With all your rage. Without remorse. Or fear.

RANI. Kalpana?

SEN. You and Kalpana. This is the first time an attack by the Indian Republican Army will be led by women.

RANI. How many? With us?

SEN. Three.

RANI. Who?

SEN. Prafulla, Panna, Mahendra.

RANI. And Craig?

SEN. He'll be there. You're brave, I've seen—

RANI. *(interrupting)* I don't need you to tell me I'm brave. I want to kill. *(beat)* Which guns?

SEN. Hmm?

RANI. Guns?

SEN. 9mm automatic pistols. Small, easy to hide.

RANI. We have enough?

SEN. Haan.

RANI. We shoot to kill.

SEN. Haan.

RANI. Craig?

SEN. Our goal is to strike fear into their hearts. This fear is far more important than killing one man, Rani.

RANI. Women, children?

SEN. What do you think?

RANI. I will. Kill them. Each and every one of them.

SEN. You can't fail.

RANI. If they catch us?

SEN. *(beat)* Cyanide. You'll all carry a capsule. You will have to disguise yourself, on the night, Rani.

RANI. I'll be a man.

SEN. What type of man?

RANI. A police officer. A collaborator. A Sikh. *(beat)* I will be a man.

SEN. This will be a great warning, Rani. Not only to the angrez. But to all those Indians who wish to become the angrez. Anglo-Indians, collaborators. All of them. We shall hit them, and the country will awaken! Bande mataram!

RANI. Bande mataram! *(beat)* Kalpana?

SEN. You'll see her in a few days —

RANI. I won't fail you. I was born for this. *(wistfully)* Time will pass. Things will change. Our country shall be free.

ACT II | SCENE 3

CHORUS. 'Time will pass, things will change, our country shall be free'! So says our heroine, Rani! And yet, my dear, dear Rani, you couldn't have been more wrong. As they say, in Hindi, 'Angrez chale gaye, aulaad chod gaye'. The British quit India, but left their children behind. Yes, mesdames et messieurs, the first prime minister of India, the great Nehru, who announced the birth of the new nation in the language of the oppressors, once claimed that he was the last white man to rule India! Imagine! And isn't our Shyamal Chatterjee a child of empire too? As Rani hurls along to her fate in 1932, Shyamal grapples with his in the 1970s. His wife and son have left him. He is alone, with Bahadur, talking to ghosts.

Shyamal, in a room. He sips a glass of whiskey. Bahadur sweeps the floor. His master is almost unaware of him.

SHYAMAL. Let me tell you a story, Ananda. Ananda? Can you hear me? Projection, projection! Ah, the power of the human voice on stage! I first went to college in this city, Ananda. In Calcutta. Years ago. I studied science, got bored and ended up sitting in on some English literature classes. English literature classes in Calcutta. Those damned classes turned out to be even more dull. Can you hear me, Ananda?

Shyamal looks around and sees Bahadur looking at him with a bemused expression.

SHYAMAL. Who are you?

BAHADUR. Bahadur.

SHYAMAL. Oh brave, mighty, fearless one!

BAHADUR. Ki?

SHYAMAL. Get up, get up. Stand...yes. Stand. You must. No, here, sit, sit. Sit on this chair. Sit.

BAHADUR. Sahib!

SHYAMAL. Sit!

Bahadur sits on the chair, the broom in his hand.

SHYAMAL. Listen to me. Where was I? Yes. In the evenings, I'd sit with some friends at the coffee-house on College Street and listen to people talk. I was young and shy and all these Calcuttans loved to talk. There was a professor by the name of Poddar, Ananda. Professor Poddar, we'd call him. Poddar was popular among the students. Always had a smile and a laugh for everyone. We became good friends, Ananda. He liked to talk and I liked to listen. He'd tell me many stories. If he had a few to drink, he'd talk about Partition. He was from Dhaka. He lost everything during Partition. Yes, Ananda, the British sliced open our country before they left. Poddar saw Hindus drop Muslim babies in pots of burning oil. He and his wife and their little son left by the skins of their teeth, taking a train to Calcutta. They came to the great infernal city with no belongings. Poddar had a cousin who helped set him up in a small flat in Chinatown. In a few weeks, Poddar got a job as a shoe salesman at a Bata store on Chittaranjan avenue. In between fitting people's shoes, he read Shakespeare at the store, to preserve his sanity. *(laughs, then halts abruptly)* On one summer's day, when the filth and poison of the city stick to you, Poddar fitted the shoes of the head of English at the university, a real Englishman he was. He knelt down, took the scrubbed white feet in dark black socks and fit the man's shoe. As he did, the Englishman glimpsed a worn-out copy of the Complete Works. He started a conversation with Poddar. A conversation about Shakespeare in a shoe store in Calcutta! Poddar had lost all his certificates of course, but perhaps in those days people believed each other, trusted each other, a little more. He was given a job as lecturer for a measly sum. He took it. He adored English. He even adored the English. Used to say we'd be running around with tails if they hadn't come along. *(beat)* He taught for a few years, became popular with the students, started to write articles in his name. Then, his wife left him, Ananda, his wife left him. His wife who had endured so much left him for one of his students. His wife who —

Pause.

BAHADUR. Jal khabe dada?

SHYAMAL. No, no water. No more —

BAHADUR. Ami jai?

SHYAMAL. No, stay here. I need an audience. *(beat)* Poddar grew bags under his eyes. His son drifted away. One day, when I sat in his little black room in his old flat in north Calcutta, a room stuffed with books, books everywhere, on the shelves, on the tables, under them, books scattered all over the floor, books covering every old bit of furniture like dust, a little boy in a white vest and red shorts entered with the news of his son's death, Ananda. He had drowned in the Ganges. No. Yes. He'd drowned. Death by dirty water! *(beat)* Poddar could do nothing but laugh. I was shocked. Poddar turned to me and said, in perfect clipped English like an Oxford don: 'I knew my son would die today.' Then, as if to prove a point, Poddar took a little, black diary, Ananda, opened it to a page and showed it to me: the date of his son's death. He'd written it down. In advance. Long before the act. I asked him how he could have possibly known. He said: 'I have suffered so much in my life, Shyamal. I can see the suffering in other faces too. I see all around me. I know when time is up.' *(He gets up on a chair and mimes trying to hang himself from the ceiling fan.)* Three days later, he hanged himself from an old, creaking ceiling fan.

Bahadur rushes to his master, and holds onto his legs as if to save him.

BAHADUR. Na, sahib, na—

SHYAMAL. Why are you stopping me?

DURGA. Na, sahib—

SHYAMAL. Chede dao. *(beat)* Let me go.

ACT II | SCENE 4

CHORUS. September 1932. A week before the attack. Rani is in Chittagong. By day, she teaches English at a local school — yes, just imagine the self-loathing! By night, she puts on her superhero outfit and makes bombs and plans to attack the Angrez, ha! Her closest friend, Kalpana Dutta, is under house arrest. Yet, from time to time, they sneak away together. And here they are, doing what they've always loved doing ever since they were children.

Chorus becomes Kalpana. During the following scene, the actors playing Rani and Kalpana mime playing badminton, while conversing with each other.

KALPANA. O baap re baap, you play a lot better these days, Rani!

RANI. Ei je, that's to be expected, na?

KALPANA. Why... why?

RANI. Because... as we... get older... we...

KALPANA. ... get wiser!

RANI. So they say!

KALPANA. Your serve.

RANI. Right. *(beat)* Ooof, terrible!

KALPANA. Try harder.

RANI. You were always... better than me... Kalpana —

KALPANA. Not bad... try harder —

RANI. Best I can do —

KALPANA. You always... take this game...

RANI. My point!

KALPANA. Too seriously —

RANI. Of course...

KALPANA. Lightness, Rani —

RANI. Not again, Kalpana —

KALPANA. Be light... it's only a game —

RANI. My point!

KALPANA. Life's a game —

RANI. My point, again!

KALPANA. See... see... good...

RANI. I wish I could —

KALPANA. What? My serve —

RANI. See life as a game —

KALPANA. Play as you sing —

RANI. That's your family wealth—

KALPANA. What?

RANI. ... speaking—

KALPANA. Not allowed...

RANI. Why? It's in, it's in...

KALPANA. Na na, no family talk please—my point! *(beat)* Pick up the shuttlecock, Rani.

Rani picks it up, drops it, picks it up again, drops it again.

KALPANA. What's wrong? You seem—I don't know—

RANI. *(nervous laughter)* Not very good with my serves—

KALPANA. Attack, Rani, attack—

RANI. *(beat)* Look out—

KALPANA. Not bad—

RANI. Good return—

KALPANA. Imagine I'm the angrez—

RANI. Hard work—

KALPANA. You can—

RANI. My point!

KALPANA. My serve. Wait. Here here, watch me—

RANI. I so wish I were you—

KALPANA. Don't talk rubbish—

RANI. You're so beautiful, Kalpana—

KALPANA. Enough enough! You're not—

RANI. My point!

KALPANA. ... going to win—

RANI. My point, Kalpana—

KALPANA. ... this way! It's not your point! I still win!

RANI. Don't rub it in, now, yes?

KALPANA. I win!

RANI. Sit?

KALPANA. Haan?

RANI. Sit.

They sit. Kalpana runs her fingers through Rani's hair.

KALPANA. I missed you.

RANI. Stop acting!

Pause.

KALPANA. What are you thinking?

RANI. I can't stand crows cawing. Look at the sky. It's gone all black, like an eclipse. As if the moon had swallowed the sun. *(beat)* You know —

KALPANA. What? Tell me.

RANI. Ready?

KALPANA. Pahartali Club?

RANI. The night of the 23rd?

KALPANA. Haan.

RANI. Craig. Governor of Bengal?

KALPANA. Haan. *(beat)* Are we ready?

RANI. I am. You don't have to... come...

KALPANA. Have you lost your mind?

RANI. I'm like your older sister, Kalpana and I don't want —

KALPANA. I'm coming with you, whether you like it or not. It's our mission. You need me.

RANI. What's the time?

KALPANA. It's getting dark. Must be close to 6.

RANI. Go home, Kalpana, it's time.

KALPANA. What?

RANI. Home. We've stayed out too long.

KALPANA. I don't feel safe. At home. I want to be with you, Masterda, all the rest, for the next week. I feel I'm being watched, Rani. I can't go.

RANI. You must, Kalpana.

KALPANA. Take me with you.

RANI. Na. If they're watching you, then you need to go home tonight.

KALPANA. I don't feel safe.

RANI. Masterda says you must go home.

KALPANA. I don't care Rani.

RANI. I say you must. And as your leader, Kalpana, I order you to go home.

Pause.

KALPANA. Feel tired. Suddenly.

RANI. And old. *(beat)* They're all gone—

KALPANA. Hmm?

RANI. Ramkrishna Da, Nirmal. All gone.

KALPANA. Did you love him?

RANI. Hmm?

KALPANA. Nirmal da. Did you —

RANI. *(beat)* I do miss him.

KALPANA. Forgive me, Rani, I shouldn't have, I didn't —

Rani suddenly reaches out to Kalpana and pulls her close.

RANI. I don't ever... want you... to leave me —

KALPANA. I won't, I —

They hold each other. Pause.

You've seen *Alam Ara*, Rani?

RANI. What?

KALPANA. The film. *Alam Ara*. In Bombay. A love story. A prince and a gypsy girl. With songs.

RANI. With songs!

KALPANA. Haan. Heard them?

RANI. Na.

KALPANA. Seen it?

RANI. Na.

KALPANA. Want to?

RANI. How?

KALPANA. *(beat)* I wish sometimes... sometimes... to run away... from Bengal.

RANI. To Bombay?

KALPANA. From all this. Masterda has been. Bombay. Says it's beautiful. A city by the sea.

RANI. Would be nice, na?

KALPANA. Haan. *(laughs)* In another life.

RANI. In another life. *(beat)* Nirmal and I... we... we dreamt of Bombay too —

KALPANA. Haan?

RANI. Haan.

KALPANA. What was it like? Your dream?

RANI. *(dreaming)* One day, we'll take the train out of Bengal. All of us. No one will ask for our papers. There'll be no sentry points, no stop and search, no different rules for whites and Indians. No one will ask us where we're from, or where we're going. In our own land. No one will treat us like dogs. We'll take the train. We'll sit in a compartment by ourselves. We'll stare out of the window at the country rushing past us, the landscape changing by the hour.

We'll talk about what we've been through, the battles we've fought, the sacrifices we've made.

KALPANA. Do you want revenge, Rani?

RANI. Hmm?

KALPANA. Revenge. For Ramkrishna Da? For Nirmal Da? For Nirmal. Your Nirmal —

RANI. Great word, na? Re-ve-n-ge! I can taste it. And it tastes of blood. The blood of the angrez! *(beat)* This is much more than revenge, Kalpana. This is about our nation's pride. The soil our farmers till. The freedom of going wherever we want, whenever we want. This is about all our people, Hindu, Muslim, Christian, Sikh. This is about our Indian sisters, who are fighting beside their brothers. This is about — *(sighs deeply)* you understand? *(beat)* You must go home now. It's getting late.

KALPANA. Don't want to —

RANI. You have to —

KALPANA. When will we —

RANI. I'll see you in a week, Kalpana. It's time.

KALPANA. *(beat)* Goodbye, Rani!

RANI. Not goodbye, Kalpana! Auf wiedersehen!

KALPANA. Baap re baap, Rani! And which language is that?

RANI. German, Kalpana. Means- 'until we see each other again'!

KALPANA. *(beat)* **Auf wiedersehen!**

ACT II | SCENE 5

Shyamal and Durga, across a table, Calcutta, late 1970s.

SHYAMAL. How long?

DURGA. Hmm?

SHYAMAL. How long has it been? Since we last saw each other?

DURGA. A year?

SHYAMAL. How is he?

DURGA. Ananda?

SHYAMAL. Who else? I don't have time for idle chatter, Durga!

DURGA. Idle chatter? You always made me laugh, Shyamal—

SHYAMAL. I haven't seen my son in a year.

DURGA. Don't blame me. You were unwell. *(beat)* I heard you were in hospital.

SHYAMAL. For a few weeks. Last year. Nothing too serious. Exhaustion.

DURGA. How are you now?

SHYAMAL. I've started work again. Back in the public sector. Easy hours. Not too much stress. Not like Bombay, you know.

DURGA. You must take care of yourself.

SHYAMAL. I've got a weak heart. And after we — *(beat)* I was tired. Felt like too many things to deal with. I was never good with stress, you know that —

DURGA. *(interrupting)* What d'you want, Shyamal? Why did you want to see me?

SHYAMAL. No, it's just that — here we are. The two of us. Back in Calcutta —

DURGA. I thought you loved this city —

SHYAMAL. What about you?

DURGA. Having my parents around makes a difference. You should know that. And Cal's a lot cheaper than Bombay.

SHYAMAL. Still teaching?

DURGA. Three days a week.

SHYAMAL. Money?

DURGA. I have enough. My parents help —

SHYAMAL. I'm tired.

DURGA. What?

SHYAMAL. No, just tired. All the time. These days. Since we —

DURGA. Why did you want to see me, Shyamal?

SHYAMAL. *(abruptly)* Why didn't *you* come to see *me*? In hospital?

Pause.

DURGA. I'm busy. I'll have to go soon.

SHYAMAL. He's starting school?

DURGA. Yes. Blue Bells, New Alipore. Nice little nursery. In an old colonial style house.

SHYAMAL. Bungalow.

DURGA. Hmm?

SHYAMAL. Bungalow. Colonial style bungalow. I think that's what you mean.

DURGA. *(beat)* Big playground for the kids. Lots of trees. Nice big classrooms in these old big rooms. You should go there sometime, see for yourself. You're paying for it.

SHYAMAL. Do you have to be so — *(beat)* We don't have to go through with the divorce.

DURGA. What? This is not the place to talk about this, Shyamal. *(beat)* I want the divorce.

SHYAMAL. It'll take years.

DURGA. I don't care. I don't want us to have —

SHYAMAL. *(interrupting)* What will people say?

DURGA. Let them say what they want—

SHYAMAL. *(suddenly)* I still miss you, Durga. Both of you. I'm sorry I—

DURGA. It takes years to get on the waiting list for some of the better schools, Shyamal, I want you to help take care of that—

SHYAMAL. Did I say I won't? *(beat)* I want him to study in St. James or St. Xavier's. Good schools where he'll get a well-rounded education. English, sciences, sports, extra-curriculars. Like I did. *(beat)* Best thing the British did in this country. Set up schools and colleges—

DURGA. To create a nation of Indian clerks to serve their Empire, na?

SHYAMAL. Without English, you're nothing today. And I'd like him to go abroad. At some point in his life. And I'll teach him all I know, Durga, I promise.

DURGA. It's a bit early for all this, na? He's only four.

SHYAMAL. No harm planning it all, Durga. I'd like him to go to England, one day—

DURGA. You really wanted to go to England, didn't you?

Pause.

SHYAMAL. What's the time?

DURGA. Hmm?

SHYAMAL. Time?

DURGA. 4.45. Don't you wear a watch?

SHYAMAL. Lost it. Somewhere. I lose a lot of things these days. *(beat)* I tried hard, Durga —

DURGA. Let's not talk about that.

SHYAMAL. Moving to Bombay three years ago. Driving thirty kilometres, each way, each day. In that traffic. In that heat. You didn't know all the pressures I was under. At one point, I was running the bank, Durga. I used to recite poetry, what was I doing working in a bloody bank? *(beat)* There's a passage in the Mahabharata which says that each of us has the freedom to either become, or not to become, oneself.

DURGA. Vah! Since when did you start taking an interest in India?

SHYAMAL. One day, I'll read them.

DURGA. What?

SHYAMAL. All our ancient books. *The Mahabharata,* the Upanishads, *Meghdutam* —

DURGA. In Sanskrit?

SHYAMAL. *(beat)* In English.

DURGA. Oh.
    Pause.

SHYAMAL. The day after you left —

DURGA. Water—

Pause. Shyamal pours Durga and himself some water. Drinks.

No whiskey?

Shyamal shakes his head.

You've given up?

SHYAMAL. I'm going on a journey.

DURGA. Where? Don't tell me? All over India?

SHYAMAL. From Kanyakumari to the Himalayas—

DURGA. My my Shyamal, from one role to another! Soon, you'll be all dressed up as a sadhu!

SHYAMAL. Funny you say that. I dreamt the other night I was on a train, and I was all dressed up in saffron. My beard was long. I wore glasses. I was nearly bald. I wore all these rings with gemstones on my fingers. And rosaries and beads around my neck. And I was talking to foreigners, white people, you know, the ones who come to India to find themselves. And I was talking to them, about India, about myself, my journey—

DURGA. *(interrupting)* I really should go, Shyamal, I'm sorry.

SHYAMAL. Stay.

DURGA. It's 5 'o clock. I have to pick up Ananda. From Maa's place.

SHYAMAL. I'll come with you.

DURGA. No, Shyamal. *(beat)* When are you off?

SHYAMAL. Hmm?

DURGA. On your great journey? All over India?

SHYAMAL. This weekend. Saturday, I think. Have to make sure. The tickets. I want this to be the beginning of something new. The first of many journeys.

DURGA. That doesn't sound like you, Shyamal.

SHYAMAL. It isn't me, Durga. I've changed.

DURGA. Good.

SHYAMAL. I want you back. Both of you, I —

DURGA. *(interrupting)* I don't have time for this. I have to go. I'm really running late.

   Pause.

SHYAMAL. Okay.

DURGA. You'll pay?

SHYAMAL. Hmm?

DURGA. The bill?

SHYAMAL. I've always fulfilled my financial obligations.

DURGA. Should I give you a medal for it?

Durga gets up to leave, Shyamal holds her by the hand.

SHYAMAL. When will I see you again?

DURGA. I don't think that's the right question, Shyamal.

SHYAMAL. What do you mean?

Pause.

DURGA. Goodbye, Shyamal.

Durga leaves.

ACT II | SCENE 6

CHORUS. On the way home after badminton, Kalpana was arrested. The angrez were waiting for her, in a jeep, hidden behind a bush, outside her home. Within a day, Rani came to know. She knew she'd never see her friend again.

Rani in front of a mirror, as in scene 1. She is dressing herself up, slowly, as a Punjabi man, with a beard and a turban.

RANI. *(mirror)* Unfortunately there are still many among my countrymen who may be shocked to learn how a woman brought up in the best tradition of womanhood has taken up such a horrible deed as to massacre human lives. I wonder why there should be any distinction between males and females in the fight for the cause? Time has come that the notion of women being weaker than men must go. We shall no more lag behind and will stand side by side with our brothers in any activities, however dangerous. My sisters will no more think themselves weaker and face all dangers and join the revolutionary movement in their thousands.

Rani turns away from the mirror, walks across the stage, and speaks to her followers.

We are fighting freedom's battle, my brothers! Today's action is part of that continued fight. British people have snatched away our independence, have bled India white and played havoc with the lives of millions of Indians, both male and female. They are the sole cause of our complete ruin — moral, physical, political and economic — and thus have proved the worst enemy of our country, the greatest obstacle in the way of recovering our independence. So we have been compelled to take up arms against the lives of any and every member of the British community, official or non-official, though it is not at all a pleasant thing to us to take the life of any human being. In a fight for freedom, we must be ready to remove, by any means whatsoever every obstacle that stands in our way.[1] Our nation awakes, my brothers! Bande mataram, long live revolution, down with imperialism! Jai Hind!

---

[1] Adapted from the official typescript of a note handwritten by Pritalata Waddedar and found on her body after the Pahartali Raid on 24th September 1932. Quoted in Chatterjee, Manini, *Do and Die: The Chittagong Uprising* (Penguin, India, 1999).

ACT II | SCENE 7

CHORUS. A week after her arrest, a British officer enters Kalpana's jail cell to tell her that her dear friend and comrade is dead. 'We did you a favour by arresting you last week', says the angrez gentleman. 'Here you are, alive and well, while your friend is as dead as a dodo.' Kalpana howls. In that empty, barren cell, she tries to imagine what had happened the previous night. She sees the Pahartali Club, Chittagong, on the night of 23rd September 1932. She hears the sounds of merriment inside — the playing of a piano, singing, the clatter of cutlery.

RANI. Time?

FIRST REVOLUTIONARY. 10.40.

SECOND REVOLUTIONARY. It's time.

FIRST REV. Yes.

RANI. Nearly. Not yet. We need —

THIRD REVOLUTIONARY. Where will I —

RANI. From the side. I'll go in from main entrance. Straight through. Wait for me to blow the whistle. Don't forget. The whistle. Understood? Five minutes. We need — *(beat)* Calm, please, each of you, be calm.

FIRST REV. I am calm.

SECOND REV. We are calm.

THIRD REV. We're all calm.

RANI. Shhh! Good. Now. Okay. Breathe, Rani, breathe. If you feel your mouth drying up, just... here... move your tongue inside your mouth... like this... trill your tongue... quietly.

SECOND REV. Throat's dry.

RANI. Move your tongue. Wets the mouth, throat, every —

FIRST REV. It does.

RANI. Shh!

SECOND REV. Why does our throat get so dry?

FIRST REV. Fear, you fool!

RANI. Quiet!

Pause.

FIRST REV. This is where Arjuna hesitated?

RANI. What?

SECOND REV. Arjuna, yes, Arjuna!

THIRD REV. Before the great battle.

FIRST REV. Long before the Buddha, deep in the shadows of time, a great warrior prince faces his family in a war of the worlds, and the moment before it starts, he hesitates. He stops. To think. He is confused. And sad. Must he fight? What's his purpose? Masterda always tells us this story.

RANI. And what do you want me to say?

FIRST REV. Nothing, nothing.

RANI. You want me to send you home. Back to your mother?

FIRST REV. Na, it's just that—

RANI. Sister?

SECOND REV. Na, just that—

RANI. Father?

THIRD REV. Na, it's just that—

RANI. Just what?

FIRST REV. Arjuna—

RANI. Quiet!

REVOLUTIONARIES *(all together)* Yes, Rani di.

RANI. Listen to them. In our own land. I hope— *(beat)* Craig is there. White monkey. *(beat)* And what does Krishna tell Arjuna?

FIRST REV. That he must fight—

SECOND REV. It's his duty—

THIRD REV. Death is passing—

FIRST REV. An illusion—

SECOND REV. Only the body—

THIRD REV. Dies!

RANI. 'I am become death, destroyer of worlds.' You have your capsules? Each of you?

REVOLUTIONARIES (*all together*): Yes, Rani di.

RANI. Good. Give me yours.

FIRST REV. What?

SECOND REV. Why?

THIRD REV. Na—

RANI. Give me your capsule. Now.

FIRST REV. Na, Rani di.

RANI. I'm a woman. I can't be captured. Do you know what they do to women?

FIRST REV. But you have yours.

RANI. Shhh!

The noise of firecrackers exploding in the distance. Laughter and voices from inside the Club. 'My word, sounded like gunfire, yes? – 'Haven't been this terrified.' – 'Bengali dogs.' – 'Ramu, ek bada peg whiskey lao.' – 'Should I have look outside?' – 'Don't worry, only firecrackers.'

RANI. Time?

FIRST REV. Hmm?

RANI. What's the time?

FIRST REV. It's 10.45.

RANI. Now!

Rani blows her whistle. Firecrackers continue exploding. The revolutionaries enter the club from the side. Grenades and gunshots. Rani shoots with her revolver. Screams from inside the club. The lights go out. Darkness. Rani lights a match. She stumbles outside with her fellow fighters. They run a little distance. She gives her guns to them.

SECOND REV. Come with us!

RANI. Go! Now! They're coming!

SECOND REV. Can't leave you he —

RANI. Go! *(beat)* Hit the enemy, hard, my brothers. Conquer him. Don't give up. This is my last wish. You have my love. Give my respects to Masterda.

They leave.

RANI. *(looking skyward)* Our martyrs are calling me.

Cries from the Club: 'Ms. Sullivan!' 'Is there a doctor here? Someone call the doctor!' Rani is alone. She has a scar of a wound on her chest.

RANI. We are fighting... freedom's battle —

She opens the capsule and drinks. Opens another. Drinks.

RANI. Bande mataram, long live—

Rani collapses.

ACT II | SCENE 8

Kolkata, 2017. Ananda is with Durga.

DURGA. How long?

ANANDA. Hmm?

DURGA. How many years?

ANANDA. Five?

DURGA. So long?

ANANDA. Thank god for Skype, haan?

DURGA. Enjoyed?

ANANDA. What?

DURGA. The food, silly.

ANANDA. Fishing for compliments?

DURGA. One tries, no?

ANANDA. Feels unreal.

DURGA. What?

ANANDA. The house. It's the same. The sofa, dining table, chairs, wooden cabinets, even the old pictures.

DURGA. I like it like that. Nothing changes. Not in this city, anyway.

ANANDA. Yah, it's like... you know... a bit of a culture shock after Bombay. What time? Tomorrow?

DURGA. Hmm?

ANANDA. Funeral?

DURGA. See that old picture with the three of us?

ANANDA. Baba's books and records in the background. Gibbon's *Decline and Fall of the Roman Empire*. He read all this?

DURGA. What do you think?

ANANDA. Still have them?

DURGA. He'd never leave his books with me. *(beat)* You were so quiet as a baby. In this house. Your father was happy. We had so many friends, you know?

ANANDA. I don't remember much.

DURGA. And in those days we were the only ones with a car. That old black Ambassador, remember? Dad had once driven that car all the way from Calcutta to Bombay and back! Imagine! Tommy uncle had a bike, but the rest, no, they just... piled onto us. Alfred, Gene, Sheshadri, Khurshid, remember them? *(beat)* Nine in the morning.

ANANDA. Hmm?

DURGA. The funeral.

ANANDA. Seen the body?

DURGA. Of course.

ANANDA. Too late tonight?

DURGA. Yes.

ANANDA. I don't know how I'll —

DURGA. Don't worry. You'll be okay.

ANANDA. When was the last time —

DURGA. What?

ANANDA. You saw him? I mean before —

DURGA. Don't remember. Years.

ANANDA. Sorry.

DURGA. For what?

ANANDA. How difficult was it, Maa? Separating? All those years ago.

DURGA. Unheard of. In those days. *(beat)* It was good that you and your father still had a relationship despite what we went through. I remember, when he used to come see us. Here. Books, music, cricket. He made you who you are today —

ANANDA. *(interrupting)* Were you scared of him, Maa?

DURGA. What?

ANANDA. Did he... raise his hands —

DURGA. I don't remember.

ANANDA. I was scared of him —

DURGA. I don't remember you being —

ANANDA. You don't want to.

DURGA. What?

ANANDA. Remember.

DURGA. Amnesia isn't a bad thing. To forget is to grow.

ANANDA. Then why didn't you?

DURGA. What?

ANANDA. Nothing.

Pause.

DURGA. Funny man, your father. In some ways, his entire life was a... I don't know... a —

ANANDA. Mistake?

DURGA. Stop it.

ANANDA. No I meant... wrong place, wrong time —

DURGA. I used to tell him he was born in England, but fell into the Black Sea. He used to hate me for it!

ANANDA. Maybe in his next life he'll be an —

DURGA. Englishman?

ANANDA. Yes!

They laugh. Pause.

Was my father a real Indian, Maa? *(beat)* Am I a real Indian?

DURGA. Come here, babu.

ANANDA. Hmm?

DURGA. Come here.

Ananda gets up and sits next to his mother. She touches his face. He puts his head on her lap.

DURGA. You're still my baby. After all these years. Sleep. You're tired.

ANANDA. The first years in England, Maa, I can't tell you, I never told you, but — *(beat)* Never mind.

DURGA. What?

SHYAMAL. I wish I could talk to Baba. Tell him what England is really like —

DURGA. Your voice, Ananda —

ANANDA. Hmm?

DURGA. Sometimes your voice sounds just like your father's.

ANANDA. Really?

Suddenly, Durga gets up and goes to a chest of drawers. Opens it, pulls out a letter.

ANANDA. Baba?

DURGA. Yes.

ANANDA. You wrote each other letters?

DURGA. He did.

ANANDA. You didn't reply?

DURGA. Sometimes.

ANANDA. Read it?

DURGA. Later. Promise. *(beat)* Strange, na?

ANANDA. What?

DURGA. He'd gone to Varanasi last year. Finally. When he knew he was dying. He'd tried once before. To travel all over India. In the 70s. I think he had a fantasy of himself as a holy man. *(laughs)* But he didn't go. He was scared. Scared of the real

India outside the cities. Like a lot of us. *(beat)* Funny, no? A man who spends his whole life dreaming of England, discovers his own country as he's dying. There's something... I don't know... something about—

ANANDA. God has a funny sense of humour—

DURGA. That's something he'd say.

ANANDA. *(beat)* Let's go to Varanasi Maa! Follow in Baba's footsteps. I've never been. I want to go. Really do. Now. Makes sense. Let's go, please. I want to!

Pause.

DURGA. *(sighs)* You must go back, Ananda. This country is not a place for you. They'll eat you alive here. They'll tear you apart, limb from limb. The wild dogs of this land. You're not tough enough to survive this place. *(beat)* Chalo, it's getting late. Have to wake up early tomorrow.

Silence. Ananda on the verge of tears.

Enough, stop this snivelling. You're a man now. *(beat)* Boys don't cry.

ACT II | SCENE 9

Tableau. Ananda circles the funeral pyre. Rani, opposite, lights a match. As Ananda watches the pyre burn, Durga comes forward with a letter.

DURGA. 'Dear Durga, Returned from Varanasi on Sunday morning. Had a fabulous trip. Reached the city at 3pm. Checked in at a guest house by the river. Walked to the famous Shiva temple. Had to walk a long way through very very narrow lanes till we reached the temple itself - quite an awesome place even with all the crowds and the dirt. From there I walked down to the river. It was around 6pm with the sun just about setting. The priests were conducting aartis to the river. Took a boat ride from the ghat for about two hours going up and down the entire length of Varanasi. It was spectacular! Great chanting of the vedic hymns by the monks. The next morning, hired a car and drove down to Sarnath where Buddha preached his first sermon. This was perhaps the icing on the cake as far as the entire trip was concerned. Was surprised to see that Sarnath has a full fledged Buddhist University with students from various Asian countries. The museum at Sarnath was spectacular. The next evening took the train and returned to Calcutta. All in all a truly wonderful trip. Inspired now to read ancient Indian History! Don't know if I have enough time. Have I wasted my life? Thinking of you. And Ananda. Have you heard from him? Does he write often? Is he eating well? Tell him to eat a lot of red meat during the winters. Red meat keeps you warm. It must be so cold in England. Love, Shyamal'

A crackling radio: Nehru's speech on India's 'tryst with destiny'. This fades into sirens and voices shouting 'Inqualab Zindabad! Down with imperialism! Bande Mataram! Jai Hind!' Ananda and Rani walk towards each other.